Location of the YOSEMITE quadrangle

High Sierra Hiking Guide #1

YOSEMITE

a complete guide
to the Valley
and surrounding uplands,
including descriptions of
more than 100 miles of trails

by the editors of
WILDERNESS PRESS
Thomas Winnett
editor-in-chief
*with Bob and
Margaret Pierce*

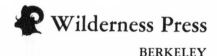 Wilderness Press

BERKELEY

1980 corrections to
High Sierra Hiking Guide #1: Yosemite

41   The Sierra Point Trail is closed as too dangerous.

43   Day Hike #8 now begins at Tamarack Flat Campground. Length is now 6 miles and 8 eq. miles; times are 3 hours down, 4 hours up.

44   The road mentioned in Line 7 is closed beyond Tamarack Flat Campground.

45   The trailhead for Day Hike #9 is at Tamarack Flat Campground. Length is now 7 miles, 11 eq. miles; times are 4 hours down, 6 hours up.

48   The trailhead is at Tamarack Flat Campground.

52   The water fountain mentioned is no longer there. The parking loop mentioned in the last line is now closed off.

55   The second sentence in the last paragraph should begin, "Soon going left (east) at a junction . . ."

67   Don't take the cross-country route up the outlet of Hart Lakes—it's too brushy.

68   Backpack Trail #2 no longer has two trailheads. Ignore the description of the "official" trailhead and find the trailhead thusly: The Chilnaulna Road starts north of a bridge across the South Fork Merced River near Wawona. Drive northeast on it to its end above Chilnaulna Creek.

Third edition copyright © 1974 by Wilderness Press

Second edition copyright © 1971 by Wilderness Press

First edition copyright © 1969 by Wilderness Press

Library of Congress Card Number 74-95768

ISBN: 911824-34-0

Manufactured in the United States

Introduction

The HIGH SIERRA HIKING GUIDES by the editors of Wilderness Press are the first *complete* guides to the famous High Sierra. Each guide covers one 15-minute U.S.G.S. topographic quadrangle, which is an area about 14 miles east-west by 17 miles north-south. The inside front cover shows the location of the quadrangle covered by this guide.

There is a great and increasing demand for literature about America's favorite wilderness, John Muir's "Range of Light." To meet this demand, we have undertaken this guide series. The purpose of each book in the series is threefold: first, to provide a reliable basis for planning a trip; second, to serve as a field guide while you are on the trail; and third, to stimulate you to further field investigation and background reading. In each guide, there are at least 100 described miles of trails, and the descriptions are supplemented with maps, mileages and other logistical and background information. HIGH SIERRA HIKING GUIDES are based on first-hand observation. There is absolutely no substitute for walking the trails, so we walked all the trails.

In planning this series, we chose the 15-minute quadrangle as the unit because—though every way of dividing the Sierra is arbitrary—the quadrangle map is the chosen aid of almost every wilderness traveler. Inside the back cover of this book is a map of the quadrangle, showing described trails and good campsites. With this map, you can always get where you want to go, with a minimum of detours or wasted effort.

It is fitting that the first guide in the series should be the guide to the *Yosemite* area. For many people, "Yosemite" is almost synonymous with "Sierra Nevada." Yosemite has been the first Sierra experience of millions of Americans, not the least—or the first—of them being John Muir. Go to Yosemite and walk the level Valley meadows, or climb the steep trails to the fabulous uplands. May this guide enhance your experience.

Sun on Half Dome after a snowstorm　　　　　*Thomas Winnett*

Table of Contents

The Country

WHETHER THE VISITOR to Yosemite National Park comes merely to see or whether he comes to experience, the country will claim him. A wonderland rich in historical background and geological wonders, it boasts a genial climate and an abundance of well-maintained trails that are an open invitation to the most casual visitor to discover for himself what lies beyond the noise and tourism of the Valley floor. Just off the trail, under the canopy of some of the world's finest forest stands, the hiker will find solitude, and in this solitude he will come to know why these national wilderness preserves are so necessary to man. It is here, in this peaceful and serene wilderness setting, that man can renew his vital sense of childlike wonder, and recreate his sense of perspective. This perspective lends depth and understanding to the story that follows.

The topographical story of the *Yosemite* quadrangle is the story of the Merced River drainage and the "Yosemite Uplands." The main trunk of the river flows east to west, originating on the slopes of the Clark and Cathedral ranges. Within the confines of this quadrangle, the Merced River enters at Little Yosemite Valley, drops over 594-foot Nevada Fall, snakes its way through the sandy sediments of Yosemite Valley, and exits through the narrow confines of Merced Gorge. Approximately 13 airline miles to the south, the South Fork of the Merced River parallels its parent stream west as far as Wawona, and then turns northwest to join the Merced River a few miles to the west of the quadrangle boundary.

None of the area within the *Yosemite* quadrangle is of the true "High Sierra." The highest point in the quadrangle is

---

Illilouette Creek *Tina Beal*

Buena Vista Peak, a mere 9709 feet in elevation; and aside
from Yosemite Valley itself there are no outstanding interior
landmarks, and no towering mountain ranges. Instead, one
may view the region lying between the Merced River and the
South Fork of the Merced River as one large rolling upland
that drops abruptly on its northern boundary into Yosemite
Valley, and nearly as suddenly on its southern boundary. To
the east, the upland butts up against the Clark Range and the
Buena Vista Crest.

Most of this upland is densely forested with pine, fir and
juniper, and only a few places show the open areas usually
associated with the Subalpine and Alpine belts of the higher
regions. Within this upland, lakes are few, what ones there are
nestling at the bases of the most prominent landforms (Horse
Ridge, Buena Vista Crest). But even as the lakes are few, they
are remote enough—a good day's walk from the nearest trailheads—to have become havens for those who seek solitude
and good fishing.

The most impressive scenery of this quad is, of course,
centered in and about Yosemite Valley. The Valley's striking
waterfalls and towering rock domes and facades draw hundreds
of thousands of visitors yearly. Most outstanding among the
Valley's landmarks are, on the north rim, Ribbon Fall, El
Capitan, Three Brothers, Yosemite Falls, Royal Arches,
Washington Column and North Dome. The south rim's major
landmarks include Leaning Tower, Bridalveil Fall, Cathedral
Rocks, Cathedral Spires, Sentinel Fall, Sentinel Rock, Glacier
Point, Vernal Fall, Nevada Fall and Half Dome.

The History

WHILE THESE LAND-marks bear the white man's labels and are the cause for his visits to the Valley, it was the Indian who gave the Valley its first names and who first appreciated its plunging waterfalls and towering rocks. The first Indians were the Ahwahneechee, a tribal branch of the western Miwok who maintained about 20 year-round villages on the Valley floor. The Ahwahneechee did appreciate and value their Valley, and the mark of their simple esteem can be seen in their myths and legends about the origins of some of the Valley landmarks.

The Legend of Too-tok-a-noo-lah

Many moons ago two bear cubs slept on a rock that grew and grew until it and they reached the sky. When the mother bear discovered their plight, she frantically assembled all of the animals of the valley to try and rescue her cubs. All of the animals, including the mighty grizzly bear, tried and failed. The assemblage was sad and despairing when along came the humblest of forest creatures, little *too-tok-a-nah* (the measuring worm). Inch by inch *too-tok-a-nah* scaled the face of the rock, and he soon surpassed the highest efforts of the forest's mightiest denizens. Day followed night and he inched his way to the top where, as legend has it, he led the two frightened and hungry cubs to safety. In the name of *too-tok-a-nah* the sons and daughters of Ahwahnee named the rock edifice *Too-tok-a-noo-lah*. (The white face calls this memorial El Capitan.)

Existing largely on the acorns that they harvested from the many oak trees in the Valley, the Ahwahneechee lived a quiet, prosaic life enlivened by an occasional bear hunt or food-finding expedition on the neighboring uplands. *A la National Geographic*, the women went topless, the children naked, and the men wore loin cloths. They lived in conical huts covered with the long, stringy bark of the incense-cedar, and they wove symmetrically designed baskets from willows and from the bark of the redbud that grew along the Merced River. These baskets saw multiple household uses, but they were also traded with the Paiutes from around Mono Lake for obsidian (arrow-heads), salt, pinyon-pine nuts and skins.

Unrecorded tribal wars and epidemics decimated the Ah-wahneechee, and the survivors deserted the Valley. Some time went by before the Indians returned, led by a young warrior of Ahwahneechee blood named *Ten-ei-ya*. With him he brought a tribal assortment numbering about 200. They called themselves the *Yo-ham-i-te* (full-grown grizzly bear). It was this group that greeted the white man.

Who the first white man was to see Yosemite Valley is still a hotly disputed question. Some argue that Joseph Walker and his party of trappers (1833), following the ridge near Crane Flat, "could not have helped but see the Valley." Most historians shrug their shoulders, saying that "it could be true, but . . ." and they cite the diary entry of W.P. Abrams (1849) as the first recorded sighting. The first recorded visit to the Valley was, as is unfortunately typical of initial white man-red man confrontations, a military one (the Mariposa Battalion). A year later the white man and the red man were killing each other, and the Yohamite were driven from the Valley. Like the grizzly bear, the Indian was considered expendable and undesirable.

The next 50 years of Yosemite history can be summed up in one word, *pre-automobile*. During this period several men whose work eventually led to the establishment of the present National Park came to the Valley. They were Galen Clark, first guardian and beloved resident; Thomas Starr King, mountaineering visitor and ardent spokesman; William H. Brewer, explorer, mountaineer and cartographer; Albert Bierstadt, painter; and John Muir, resident conservationist and mountaineer. By 1890, national-park status was accorded Yosemite, and substantial deletions and additions were made in 1905 and 1930.

In 1900 the first automobile entered the Valley, and tourist visitations mounted to over 33,000 by 1915, over 200,000 by 1925, and 2,303,800 by 1972. The advent of the automobile and the consequent building of roads has made Yosemite one of the most heavily visited national parks in the U.S., and recent planning by Park officials has reviewed the attendant problems of air pollution, noise and misbehavior, with an eye to banning the automobile from the Valley floor.

By 1914 most of the major roads and backcountry trails had been established. This date also marked the official turnover of Park authority from the military to civilian administration. Although some people decry "the military mind," the Army administration of the Park was a time of paternalistic progress. Maintaining headquarters at Wawona (and later in the Valley), the Army built many new trails for patrolling the Park, and today's hiker will frequently run across the T-blaze marking these old routes.

Initially there was some grumbling at being posted "in the
boondocks," but the discontent disappeared as the men and
officers began to take an interest in the natural challenges of
this scenic region. Evidence of this interest can still be seen in
the arboretum signs left over from their encampment at Wawona, on the southwest side of the river, across from Wawona
Campground. But the marks of human habitation of the land,
like those of Army occupation, are fleeting. Time erases it all,
and when man is gone there will be a new clock—the clock of
the rocks.

. 515—The First House, in the Yo Semite Valley, Ca

The Parks

BECAUSE ALMOST ALL THE territory covered in this book is under National Park Service juris-
diction, readers should know some of the present and future
plans of those who manage this park, where one can still see
and enjoy some of the wilderness that was America's heritage.
Since our ever-increasing population has taken over all but a
small portion of the original wilderness, what remains is priceless, for wilderness cannot be made—we can only save what we
have.

The National Park Service has been assigned the responsi-
bility to regulate the use of these lands so as to leave them
unimpaired for the enjoyment of future generations—as well
as to make them available to the present generation. The Park
Service develops areas for public use, including campgrounds,
stores, hotels, restaurants and service stations, and when these
become overcrowded it is pressured to expand the developed
areas. Yet making these areas ever larger for more people will
eventually ruin the values that led to their development in the
first place. The answer seems to be some kind of rationing of
the time and space that any one person is allowed to use in a
national park.

For years this has been done in Yosemite Valley, by dividing the campgrounds into definite camp spaces and limiting
the time a space can be used by any camper. In the backcountry wilderness areas, ways are being devised to reduce the
harmful effects of too many people in one area. Wilderness
permits are required for overnight camping, and one may
build wood fires only in designated areas—although chemical
stoves may be used anywhere. The size of groups allowed into

the backcountry is also being restricted. Check with the Park
Service before planning a trip with a group of more than seven
people. Overused and worn-out areas may be closed to use, so
they can recuperate and return to something like their original
condition. In any event, wood fires are not allowed above
9600 feet elevation anywhere in the Park, because of the
scarcity of wood there.

Another concern of the Park Service is the conduct and
manners of visitors. The constant increase in number of visitors to the backcountry requires that they conduct themselves
differently than their predecessors did. No longer can one cut
small branches or growing things to make a soft bed. In many
areas where wood is scarce, it is urged (in some places required) that no wood fires be used. A stringent necessity is
that all refuse be carried out. If bottles, cans and foil con-
tainers can be carried *in* full, they certainly can be carried *out*
empty. Backpackers generally do not carry many cans or
bottles, but some food packages are wrapped in foil, and foil
is becoming an eyesore at many campsites. Backcountry
travelers using pack animals are more likely to carry cans and
bottles and, of course, they should be sure to carry them out—
and also any left by their careless predecessors.

To help prevent pollution, camp at least 100 feet (200 feet
is better) from any stream, lake or trail. If there are campsites
closer than that, help by obliterating them. Where there are
no toilets, go well away from streams, lakes, trails and campsites and leave no sign. Do not wash yourself or your equipment in a stream or lake, and don't throw soapy water on its
banks. Leave your campsite clean no matter what its condition when you arrived.

The Geology

IF ONE CAN ACCEPT the idea that time "passes" quickly or slowly, depending on who is marking it, then it is an easy, yet profound step to an acceptance of the thousand-year seconds of the ponderous clock of geologic history. To the rocks, time is measured in millions of years, and man is a mere transient moth beating frantic wings against the light of historical perspective. This concept may bother man, but it fazes the rock not at all.

As nearly as can presently be determined, the earth's rock is 4.5 billion years old—and an ancestral Sierra Nevada range rose from a shallow inlet arm of the Pacific Ocean about 130 million years ago. When one is talking in terms of the geologic clock, this spectacular upthrust of rock might be called "sudden." For several million years the "skin" of the earth, succumbing to unknown pressures, folded and crumpled, creating a series of ridges separated by troughs and basins. At the same time, far below the earth's skin, a tumorlike bubble of gases and molten rock pressed upwards and formed perhaps 100 buried granite domes, or plutons, collectively called the great Sierra batholith.

For a period of a few geologic heartbeats the mountains rested and were eroded down to gentle, small hills. But the restless earth lifted and squeezed the Sierra rocks several times more in the last 60 million years. By 5 million years ago much of the great batholith had been exposed to the surface by erosion of the overlying rocks. Then, beginning only 2 million years ago, there ensued a series of short, violent upthrusts, and a corresponding down-dropping of the Owens Valley. The Sierra crest rose several thousand feet, creating a tilted block with a severe eastern scarp and a gentle slope toward the west. This is roughly the way it remains today, but one should not disregard the fact that the geologic clock continues to tick.

The brief "instant" since this uplifting and downfaulting began (about 2 million years) seems almost too ephemeral to mention, but it was during this "instant" that rivers of ice sculpted and scoured the dramatic landforms of the present-day Sierra. It was then that the marvels of Yosemite Valley and the forested country to the south were carved, polished and washed by ice and water.

By the ticking of the geologic clock man has trod the historic rock of the Sierra but microseconds. Man's appearance brought wonder—wonder at the scale of the mountains, and wonder about their origin. As late as 1913, controversy raged between 12 theorists over the origin of Yosemite Valley, and foremost among these wonderers were Josiah Whitney and John Muir. Whitney contended that the Valley was the product of a downfaulting of the earth's crust; Muir believed that glaciers were responsible. Muir was vindicated by the work of Francois E. Matthes.

Matthes, through diligent field work (Professional Paper #160, U.S. Geological Survey, 1930), discovered that the Yosemite Glacier at one time completely filled Yosemite Valley and spilled over the rim onto the adjoining highland areas. (Evidence indicated that Glacier Point was, at one time, as much as 500 feet below the glacier's surface.) Matthes concluded that the glaciers advanced and receded at least three times in the Valley, cutting and "plucking" into the jointed rock until they left a deeply incised U-shaped profile (in cross section). It is interesting to note that the depth of the glaciers is not to be judged by the present-day floor of the Valley. The bedrock that lay at the bases of the glaciers is as much as 2000 feet below the present Valley floor—underneath the Ahwahnee Hotel—the Valley floor being sediments deposited after the last glacial stage. These glaciers altered the topography considerably by shearing away whole ridge spurs, and depositing mountainous piles of debris called moraines.

Despite this awesome power, the Yosemite glacier was, as Matthes pointed out, the smallest trunk glacier in the central Sierra Nevada, and, at its longest, was scarcely 36 miles in length. But what it lacked in scale it more than made up for in dramatic effects. Joined by the feeder glaciers from the drainages of the Tenaya, Illilouette, Bridalveil and Yosemite creeks, the *mer de glace* concentrated on the vertical joints of the valley slopes and carved what Matthes has rightly called "The Incomparable Valley."

Even as it is important what was quarried, it is equally important what was left. The spectacular rock landmarks of Yosemite Valley resisted the attacks of the glaciers because they were the least-jointed rocks in the canyon, and hence the least susceptible to the ice-cracking, lifting and plucking by which the Yosemite glacier system did its work. On El Capitan and the other major columns, glacial action was restricted primarily to rasping and polishing because of the massive, unjointed face presented to the ice—it couldn't get a "hold."

Equally renowned as landmarks left by the glaciers are the Valley's waterfalls. Best known among these falls are Yosemite, Bridalveil and Nevada. Each of these waterfalls resulted when a smaller feeder glacier deepened its valley less fast than the Yosemite trunk glacier deepened the main valley. When the ice melted, these tributary valleys were left "hanging" high on the brim of the main valley; they are, appropriately enough, called hanging valleys. One of these hanging valleys, the Merced River drainage, has hanging valleys of its own (Starr King Meadows, and several unnamed valleys on the side of the Clark Range). Other hanging valleys along the rim of Yosemite Valley are watercourses for Ribbon Creek, Meadow Brook, Sentinel Creek, Illilouette Creek, and Indian Creek, and though the volume of water in any of these streams does not equal that of Yosemite Creek, Bridalveil Creek or the Merced River (some are dry by mid-summer), they do provide scenic silver ribbons for spring photographers, and water for thirsty hikers traversing the Valley uplands.

Although evidence of the glacial age is most marked in the Valley, backcountry travelers who have walked or ridden the triangular-shaped uplands between the Merced River and its South Fork know by the telltale evidence of moraines, striae, erratics and polish that the ice mantle covered most of this upland area. But unlike the High Sierra to the east, this area has no glaciers hanging on the sides of lofty peaks, and the relatively mild glaciation that this upland experienced left it with enough topsoil for the dense forest cover that presently mantles it.

"We are thus living in the period of big cities. Deliberately, the world has been amputated of all that constitutes its permanence: nature, the sea, hilltops, evening meditation." A. Camus, *The Myth of Sisyphus.*

The Fauna

THE DENSE FOREST COVER with its attendant lush plant life has made the uplands the haven they are for Sierra fauna. Birdlife in particular abounds in these amenable climes, and whether one is on the trail or merely loafing about camp, one will likely see jays, robins, chickadees, nuthatches, juncos, hummingbirds, grosbeaks, warblers, sparrows, blackbirds and hawks. Unfair as it may seem to the hearty walker, the Valley camper, without any effort at all, will see a large portion of the bird population, because the birds have adapted to the "easy pickings" of the Valley restaurants and camp tables. Certain birds, however, prefer the less populated backcountry—owls, quail, grouse, nutcrackers, eagles and ouzels. Hence those who walk will glean the rewards of some exclusive sightings.

The backcountry walker will also benefit from sightings of the abundant mammal population in their natural settings. Mule deer with their large, mulelike ears are a common sight around meadow fringes early in the mornings and late in the afternoons. Their twin, pear-shaped tracks are the most frequently seen and identified spoor in the Sierra, and a century of mountaineers have shared an admiration for the deer's grace and agility when, through dense timber, they make their head-high flight from danger. Meadow edges are choice places for observing deer, but they are also the home of the Belding ground squirrel, pocket gopher and white-footed deer mouse. Consequently they are also the hunting habitat of the great horned owl and various hawks. Hikers with the time and patience will usually be rewarded for their efforts if they plan their lunch breaks alongside meadows like Peregoy, McGurk or

Pothole (adjoining the Glacier Point Road). At the expense of some shoe leather, one can take up remoter observation stands on the fringes of meadows like Ribbon and Eagle (on the north uplands), and Turner, Lost Bear and Johnson Lake (on the south uplands).

Less commonly seen in the backcountry, but by far the most discussed animal, is the black bear. Because the bear is the largest of the mammals here (up to 5 feet in length and 300 pounds in weight), and because the animal is known to eat meat, it is the object of all manner of irrational fears. Unlike the grizzly bear (ironically the state symbol, despite the fact that the species has been extinct in California for over 50 years) the black bear is not normally pugnacious or ferocious—unless threatened. **It is foolhardy to threaten or tease any wild animal.** *Black* is a generic term for this bear, for in coloring it varies from black to cinnamon-brown. Both the young and the adult bears are adept climbers, and when frightened will frequently take to the trees. Normally of placid temperament, the black bear can turn ugly for two reasons: threats (imagined or real) to its young and threats to ist food supply. If a bear claims food that has been left within its reach, it considers this food personal property worthy of defense.

So much for the normal bear, for it is not the normal bear that is the problem in national parks and backcountry areas of high human impact. The problem is the "camp bear." One observer described this black bear as a "dyspeptic pensioner," and his description is accurate. Black bears of Yosemite Valley that depend upon gleanings from campers cannot be expected to be of the best disposition. Certainly it is not reasonable to blame the animal. Park policy is to provide a method of garbage disposal that will eliminate these "pensioners." The cause, availability of food, is correctable, but the solution also requires the cooperation of the car camper and the high-country backpacker. Car campers should keep all food closed inside their cars. Backpackers walking likely camp-bear country (i.e., heavily used backcountry trails) should forgo fresh meats and other attractive goodies, and learn the proper method of bearbagging. When you get your wilderness permit, you will be given literature describing the counterbalance method of bearbagging. Follow these instructions. In some backcountry locations that are especially popular, steel cables have been strung between two trees for you to put your rope over. Be *very* careful to follow the instructions for raising and lowering these cables; otherwise the bears may get your— and everyone else's—food.

As the camp bear is a Valley curiosity, so is the summertime horde of Valley fishermen. One cannot help speculating that the fish in the Merced River are outnumbered by the anglers 10 to 1. Certainly the fine fishing waters on the upland regions above the rim of the Valley should draw more fishermen than they do. The 12 lakes around the Buena Vista Crest and Horse Ridge are prolific fish producers, yet they are among the least visited in this quadrangle. Here fishermen will find the square-tailed eastern brook trout, the multihued rainbow trout and the olive-backed, red-dotted brown trout. To the north, anglers may enjoy solitary fishing on Yosemite and Porcupine creeks. Despite the heavy foot traffic along the upper reaches of the Merced River, fishermen will find the holes there populated by eastern brook, cutthroat and rainbow trout.

The Flora

THE FINE TROUT PROPAGA-
tion in these upland streams is the
result of clean, clear streams and
lakes. But equally important is the abundance of food, a fact
that directly relates to the presence of a healthy ground cover
and rich humus soil layer. The southern uplands are, in particular, blessed with a fine forest cover. Here backcountry
travelers will encounter mature stands of trees, ranging from
the lower pine-oak woodland belt to the dense coniferous forests of the ponderosa and lodgepole pine belts. Southeast of Wawona, just north of the quadrangle border, one can even wander
through one of the last remaining groves of giant sequoias
(Mariposa Grove). These trees with their massive trunks dwarf
all the other flora in the quad, and, like the geologic clock,
place the human viewer in a better ecological perspective.

Appreciation of the trees of Yosemite does not, however,
depend upon mere size—although truly mature trees have become the exception rather than the rule in the Sierra today,
owing to severe harvesting by the lumber industry. The term
pine tree covers, in the *Yosemite* quad, seven of the eight pine
species found in the Park. Two of these, the digger and the
knobcone, grow mostly in the lower foothill belt, but examples of each can be seen on the slopes beside the Arch Rock
entrance station.

The most commonly found pines of the *Yosemite* quad are
the ponderosa and the Jeffrey. Fine examples of the ponderosa pine can be viewed along the Valley floor, where it is
mingled with mature incense-cedars, black oaks and occasional
Jeffrey pines. It is the most widely distributed of all North
American pines, and is often mistaken for its close relative,

the Jeffrey pine. (Fine examples of the latter can be seen near Glacier Point and in the flats of Little Yosemite Valley.) However, even the weekend naturalist can tell these two trees apart by their cones. The prickle (the sharp tip at the end of each cone scale) of the larger Jeffrey-pine cone is turned *inward*, while the prickle of the ponderosa pine is turned *outward*. Should the fruit of the tree be unavailable for inspection, one can, with a minimal loss of dignity and circumspection, apply the "nose test." This consists of inserting one's nose into a seam in the bark, and inhaling deeply. A vanilla fragrance assures the pitchy-nosed detective that the tree in question is indeed a Jeffrey pine, while no identifiable odor should assure him it is a ponderosa.

Higher on the upland slopes, one will encounter the lodgepole pine, the next-most-common pine in the quad. This pine comes in nearly pure stands, and is readily identifiable by its scaly, thin bark and its two-needle cluster (it is the only two-needle pine in Yosemite). Pure stands of this tree, particularly of younger trees, are frequently so dense as to be almost impenetrable. As the grove matures, however, competition culls out the less-healthy trees. This tree has been called a "meadow murderer" with some justification. The lodgepole is the first tree to infringe on the Subalpine grasslands, and over a period of many years it takes over a meadow.

Two other pines found in this quad have many similar physical characteristics, and are sometimes mistaken for each other—the sugar pine and the western white pine, or silver pine. Both grow to about the same girth; their barks are, at first glance, similar; and they both have short, five-needle clusters of a bluish-green color. The most distinctive difference between them is in their cones. The sugar-pine cone is the granddaddy of them all, frequently attaining a length of 16 inches. The cone of western white pine, on the other hand, seldom exceeds 8 inches. The barks also differ: the bark of the mature sugar pine has *predominant* vertical furrowing; that of the mature western white pine has no distinctive furrowing, but displays a checkerboard effect.

It should be noted that *Yosemite* quad has one of the few remaining virgin sugar-pine forests of the world. Although there are larger stands in the northwest section of the Park, the Little Yosemite Valley stand is, by virtue of its lovely setting, one of the most memorable in the Park.

For native beauty no stand of timber exceeds a stand of red fir. This symmetrical tree is commonly known to the city dweller as the "silvertip" Christmas tree, but to the woodsman it is known as "the green cathedral." Because stands of red fir are relatively pure and their foliage dense, forest visitors are always struck by the shaded stillness that attends them. Here only filtered light penetrates, and the heady aroma of pitch is everywhere. Walking below these trees' densely foliated crowns is, as one famous mountaineer put it, "an experience in serenity."

Beyond the red fir's esthetic value, it is a provident source of wood for the backcountry camper. Relatively brittle, it is

"To me the meanest flower that blows can give
Thoughts that do often lie too deep for tears."   Wordsworth

easily snapped off by wind and snow. Hence the winter "fall" of the red-fir forest is typically a fine camp wood supply. The bark is also much sought after as a source for coals, and is used in place of charcoal by woodsmen. Dense stands of this tree can be found along the Panorama Trail near Glacier Point, and along Bridalveil Creek in the southern uplands.

The white fir is a common neighbor of the red fir. Usually occurring at a slightly lower elevation than the red fir, the white fir is often mistakenly identified as red. With younger trees, whose bark has not yet acquired its distinctive hues, this error is understandable, but a close examination of the needles of both young and mature trees should make the identification easy. Each needle of the white fir has a distinctive half-twist at the base where it joins the twig; the red-fir needle does not.

The Douglas-fir grows between 3500 and 5500 feet, in spotty stands. It occurs singly or in small groups associated with almost all the other conifers of the Park. Despite its designation, the Douglas-fir is not a true fir, and the various names by which the tree has been called (Douglas spruce, yellow fir, Oregon pine, false hemlock) are evidence of the confusion that attends its identification. This tree can achieve heights greater than the giant sequoia, but none of these record colossi grace the Park. A sure identification of this tree can be made by examining its abundant cones. These tiny cones possess a distinctive three-pointed, papery bract that protrudes between scales.

Among the other cone-bearing trees found along the trails described here are the incense-cedar and the California torreya. The former is by far the more common, and along the Valley floor it is the second-most-abundant conifer. It is distinguished by its cinnamon-red, deeply fissured, vertically slabbed bark and its yellow-green, platelet-spray branchlets. The California torreya is sometimes called the California nutmeg because of its fruit's resemblance to the tropical spice. In profile it very much resembles the Douglas-fir, but close scrutiny of the flat, lance-shaped needles and the blue-green, nutlike cones quickly differentiates them. This is a very rare tree in the Park, but isolated examples can be seen near the Arch Rock entrance station, near Cascade Creek along the Old Big Oak Flat Trail (Day Hike #9) and near the Wawona Tunnel.

No survey of the forest cover would be complete without mention of the broad-leaved trees. These include the black oak, white alder, black cottonwood, willows, California laurel (bay), bigleaf maple, Pacific dogwood, Oregon ash and California buckeye. There are several other deciduous trees that were introduced to the Valley by settlers, but they are of restricted and isolated incidence. The quaking aspen is not a resident of the Valley floor, but may be seen along streams of the uplands (including points near Bridalveil Creek along the Glacier Point Road).

HAIKU
"Wake! The sky is light!
Let us to the road
Again . . .
Companion butterfly."   Basho

Fleecy cumulus clouds sometimes herald rainshowers

The Climate

MAN, LIKE THE REST OF the biota with which he shares the land, depends upon the climate. Of particular interest to visitors to Yosemite Valley and the uplands are the rain forecasts. These forecasts are posted at the visitor center in Yosemite Village and at the Wawona Ranger Station; backcountry travelers can combine their last-minute weather queries with getting a wilderness permit (required). Since most backcountry travelers make their treks during the summer months, there is less concern with the winter's precipitation, but, as most experienced mountaineers already know, the previous winter's snow accumulation can affect both the summer's precipitation rate and the temperatures (not to mention the accessibility of the high country). Large snowpacks can delay the arrival of spring, and make many summer nights very cold indeed.

Generally, however, Sierra summers are remarkably dry, and, in the Transition life zone (this includes Yosemite Valley), days are normally hot as well as dry. This weather contrasts sharply with the more genial climate of the forested uplands, the Canadian life zone. When rain does fall during the summer months, it is likely to take the form of light afternoon showers, but even the most optimistic backcountry hiker carries a plastic tarp as insurance.

Lightning during these quick summer thundershowers is a danger to be reckoned with, and visitors to the Park should observe the following precautions during lightning activity. 1) Avoid being "conspicuous": stay clear of open expanses of water; keep off open expanses of rock or meadow; and stay away from outstanding landmarks such as lone, isolated trees.

2) Seek shelter and stay put until the storm is well past. One's car is a good, safe place from which to watch a storm's progress. If in the backcountry, seek out shelter in dense tree stands that have a consistent configuration, with no outstanding trees.

But to precede the reader's visit to Yosemite National Park with dire warnings and a list of *do*s and *don't*s is to destroy that prized and infinitely fragile element of the wilderness experience called *discovery*. Too much foreknowledge can be almost as deadly as too little, but if one is to err, it is, perhaps, better to err on the side of precaution. We go to wilderness to discover what there is to be seen and felt, and return to find that the discovery was within ourselves—that a profound learning took place which brought a new sense of perspective.

Merced River, Sentinel Rock   *Jeff Schaffer*

The Trails

IN THIS AGE OF MAN AS The Great Spectator, there is an urgent need for physical involvement and commitment. The glass and steel of the modern-day automobile stands between man and the country, and if any real perspective is to be acquired in this country, man must emerge from his mechanical cocoon and walk the trails.

The trails and routes described in this guide vary greatly in length, underfooting, amount and steepness of ascent and descent, nearby scenery and distant views; but they can be classified in three categories: **day hikes, backpack trails and lateral trails.** The day hikes vary in length from an easy 3 miles to a tough 17 miles. Some of the longer day hikes can also be taken as easy backpack trips, and anyone in excellent physical condition can do some of the backpack trips as day hikes. Some of the backpack trips are only overnighters, but by combining trails one could devise a month-long trip. Lateral trails are connecting trails between two backpack trails.

The trails of Yosemite traverse a park that is world-renowned for its spectacular beauty, and each turn of the path brings a new and different scene. The trails on the Valley floor are mostly level, requiring only a small amount of energy for short walks, and walks of any length can be put together using the many trails there. The two roads that parallel Yosemite Valley on the nearby uplands have ideal starting points for day-hikers who are looking for easy downhill walks that can be done in one day. Crossing the north uplands is the Tioga Road; close to the south rim is the Glacier Point Road. Several hikes in this guide start from trailheads on these roads, and a public bus makes a trip on each road every day during the summer.

Reservations are necessary. For fares and schedule write to
Yosemite Transportation System, Yosemite, CA 95389.

One of the rewards of backpacking is being able to leave the
trail and go cross-country. Only one cross-country route is
described in this book (part of Backpack Trail #3). A large
part of this quad is heavily forested—not the best terrain for
cross-country hiking. However, if one does not mind a little
bushwhacking, and one has sufficient experience, one can
plan other cross-country trips in *Yosemite.*

For help in planning hikes, consider the following. With
a pack of about 1/5 your body weight you can expect to
cover two horizontal miles per hour. Add one hour for each
1000 feet of elevation gain. If you are going 12 miles, and
the total of all the "ups" is 1500 feet, you can expect to be
walking for about 6 hours plus 1½ hours = 7½ hours. This
includes normal rest stops.

We see that 1000 feet of elevation gain is the equivalent
in time and effort of two miles of horizontal walking. Taking
this relation into consideration, this book gives the *equivalent*
miles ("eq. miles") as well as the trail miles for all hikes that
have more than 500 feet of elevation gain.

For downhill walking, use the figure of two miles per hour
except where the trail is very steep. A very steep section will
require an extra hour for 2000 feet of descent.

If you are walking without a pack, or you are in really excellent condition, you can go faster—perhaps up to 50% faster.

If you are walking cross-country, it may take you all day
to go just two miles. There is a wide variation, depending on
the slope, the footing, the ground cover, your physical condition, and your acclimation to the altitude.

Trail Descriptions

(The route descriptions that follow often mention "ducks" and "ducked routes." A duck is one or several small rocks placed in an obviously non-natural way. "Eq. miles" is explained in the previous chapter. Differences in elevation are expressed in feet; horizontal differences are given in yards or miles. The time required for a hike assumes you are in good health and modestly fit.)

DAY HIKE #1

Camp Curry to Happy Isles and return via the stables (3 miles) 2-4 hours

Happy Isles is both a beauty spot and the site of an informational nature program. At the exhibit building at Happy Isles there are wildlife displays, a beautiful slide show with comments taken from John Muir's writings, and talks by rangers knowledgeable about backpacking.

The trail starts at Curry Village, proceeds past the parking lot and the tent-cabin area, and just beyond passes an open area on the right that is now used as an overflow parking lot. Here the blacktop path leads toward the shuttlebus roadway, but if you prefer a more secluded route to Happy Isles, proceed through this overflow parking area. On the far side an unmarked trail takes off and a few yards farther picks up some power lines, which it follows to Happy Isles. This little-used trail stays closer to the Glacier Point "apron" but is never far from the roadway. It is well shaded by black oaks, incense-cedars and a few ponderosa pines; but some breaks in the forest do permit glimpses of the solid cliffs close by on the right and, higher up, Glacier Point, with its distinctive gray streak where the firefall used to come down and burn off the lichen. You can even see the Point's much photographed overhanging rock. A half mile from Camp Curry is the Junior Ranger Training Program area, where children come in the summer to learn about wildlife. Proceed through the training area and across a well-used trail which is strictly a horse trail (pedestrians not allowed). Beyond the horse trail a wooden walkway negotiates a swampy area before we arrive at the old Happy Isles parking area, no longer used by cars. Turn right to the exhibit building and spend a little time there. Leaving the building, walk directly toward the river and cross the wooden footbridge to one of the Happy Isles. After exploring its beauty, continue across another footbridge and climb a few steps to the John Muir Trail, blacktopped in its initial miles here. A few steps up this trail, a flowing spring furnishes deliciously cool spring water, and here also the steep trail to Sierra Point (Day Hike #7) takes off. However, your route turns left at the junction and goes downhill to the beginning of the John Muir Trail. Here is a stream-gauging station, where exhibits show the effects of water on the environment. Instruments here measure the flow of the Merced River at this point. Amble down the right bank of the river, passing through a short tunnel under a roadway. The trail stays close to the river, and one can observe how the stream bed has changed in recent years, forming some small islands and killing a few large ponderosa pines, which cannot survive with constantly wet feet. The low, sandy, rocky hill where the trail turns left away from the roadway is a medial moraine, formed by the joining of the great Merced and Tenaya glaciers. At the lower end of the moraine we cross the Merced River on Clark's Bridge and return to Camp Curry through the parking area. Here is an old apple orchard which, in the spring during blossom time, is a delightful place to stroll; in the fall an occasional bear may be seen up in a tree trying to beat humans to the fruit.

DAY HIKE #2

Stables to Mirror Lake and return (3½ miles)
2-4 hours

This trip to a well-known and popular spot takes a route that only a few visitors use.

The trail from the stables starts down Tenaya Creek and skirts the North Pines campground. A quarter mile downstream it turns right across a bridge over Tenaya Creek and goes through the Group Campground. Across the bicycle roadway is a trail junction where the left fork goes to the Village area and our route to Mirror Lake goes right (east). The trail, well shaded by large ponderosa pines, incense-cedars, black oaks, live oaks and Douglas-firs, winds among huge blocks of granite which have fallen from the cliffs. Where the forest thins, one can look up the sheer vertical wall of Washington Column. Across the canyon is world-famous Half Dome. A

half mile from the last trail junction we come to the Indian
Caves area, a good place for a family picnic, for children love
to scramble over, under and between the large granite blocks.

The trail passes close to a shuttlebus stop before it starts
its gradual climb to Mirror Lake. This ascent is a delightful
part of the trail, and one should take the time to enjoy the
beauty all around. The birds are usually singing, large gray
squirrels scamper about, and from time to time the forest permits new views of the surrounding Valley walls. North Dome
appears on the left, and one of the Quarter Domes is seen just
up-canyon from Half Dome. After a short climb among
granite blocks, the trail drops down to the roadway and then
to Mirror Lake. Early morning is best for photographing the
lake, when it is smooth and the morning light makes fine
shadows and reflections.

From the lake we go down-canyon about 200 yards, cross
a small footbridge over Tenaya Creek and take the trail downstream on the other side. The short descent here is moderately steep, but soon we come to a flat area which is the head
of Yosemite Valley. A few more minutes of walking bring us
to the Tenaya Creek roadway bridge and another trail junction.
The trail down the creek takes one directly to the stables, but
the slightly longer route is more interesting.

Taking the left fork at the junction, we soon climb the
medial moraine formed about 10,000 years ago by the Tenaya
and Merced glaciers, which merged here and dropped some of
the rocks, pebbles and sand they had carried down their respec-
tive canyons. After crossing the crest of this moraine, descend
and cross the roadway, then turn right (west) down the Merced
River. After one-fourth mile, cross the roadway to the stables.

DAY HIKE #3

Mirror Lake to Snow Creek and return (3½ miles)
2-4 hours

This trip up lower Tenaya canyon passes through a shady forest beside a creek whose moods vary from quiet to boisterous. The destination is a little-visited tributary stream that leaps down from the high country. From the shuttlebus stop at Mirror Lake go down to the lake, turn left and skirt the north shore. Early morning is usually best for seeing and photographing the reflections for which this lake is famed. Later, breezes erase the mirror images. The granite dome on the north side of the canyon is Mt. Watkins, and on the south side Half Dome is easily recognized. The meadow at the lake inlet is worth more than a passing glance. The lake once covered this area, but it has filled in with sand and mud brought down by Tenaya Creek. Eventually the entire lake will fill in, making a larger meadow. Then trees will grow in the meadow, and it will be forest. This is the inexorable sequence of change throughout mountain country in the absence of natural or man-made interruptions. However, Mirror Lake has such scenic qualities and is visited by so many people that Park authorities feel part of it should be perpetuated, so they have dredged some sand and silt from the lower end, and will probably continue to do so periodically.

From the meadow we stroll up the undulating trail beneath black oaks and live oaks, incense-cedars, ponderosa pines, Douglas-firs and California bays. There are many young cedars and pines, but only old oak trees, because the Yosemite

Indians set fires periodically to burn out the shrubs and the young trees. This allowed the sun-loving oaks to propagate, which they have not been able to do in the dense shade of recent years. Acorns were one of the Indians' staple foods.

About a mile up this trail, the Snow Creek Trail takes off on the left to climb out of the canyon to North Dome and then to the Tioga Road. Ten or fifteen minutes spent climbing a short distance up this trail will take you above the trees and reward you with marvelous views up and down the canyon and across to the sheer face of Half Dome. From this junction one-quarter mile beside now-rushing, noisy Tenaya Creek brings us to another junction. A short quarter mile up the left-hand trail is Snow Creek, but this trail has been abandoned as too dangerous.

Returning to the main trail, we cross a bridge over Tenaya Creek and turn downstream on the south side. The trail here passes through some dense forests that are quiet, shady and cool, and delightful on a hot summer day. We again pass the meadow above Mirror Lake, then continue around the east and south sides of the lake. About a quarter mile below the lake is a footbridge leading to the roadway, where one can go a quarter mile up to the Mirror Lake bus stop or a quarter mile down to the Indian Caves bus stop.

HAIKU

"One fallen flower
Returning to the
Branch? . . . Oh no!
A white butterfly."   Moritake

DAY HIKE #4

Camp Curry to Yosemite Falls via southside and return via northside (5 miles)
2-4 hours

Although this easy walk leads through the most populated parts of Yosemite Valley, only in short sections is the trail crowded.

Going west from the main building of Camp Curry, we pass the camp cabin area and continue through an open forest of ponderosa pine, incense-cedar, black oak and maple. The Sierra Club's Le Conte Memorial Lodge is a quarter mile beyond the cabins, and a stop here is worthwhile to see the exhibits and to inspect the fine mountaineering library. Across the roadway is the housekeeping section of Camp Curry. There are two trails from Le Conte Lodge—the blacktop footpath next to the road and the bridle path a few yards up toward the cliffs.

Continuing west and keeping to the bridle path as it veers left, away from the road, one finds oneself in a near wilderness of rocks and forest for a few moments. About 1.25 miles from the start is a side road and a parking lot for the Valley chapel and Pohono Masonic Lodge. Turn right on this road, pass by the chapel, and beyond the main road find the foot trail leading across the lovely meadow. The grandeur of Yosemite Falls is before you all the way across.

Midway in the meadow we cross the Merced River on the superintendent's bridge; his house is just beyond, at the north edge of the meadow. As you near the main road, keep right,

cross it, and take the trail into the forest beyond. About 100
and 150 yards from the road are two bridges over Yosemite
Creek. Just before you cross the second bridge, the bridle path
turns right, missing the close approach to the lower fall.
Across the second bridge is the falls parking lot and a well-
traveled footpath with an outstanding view of the falls. Tilt-
ing your head back to look up, you see the feathery upper fall,
just below it a fall in the middle cascades, and then the thun-
dering lower fall! It may help you to comprehend the great
height of Yosemite Falls if you know that the lower fall alone
is twice as high as Niagara Falls. During the spring runoff,
spray from the falls sweeps right over the bridge near the base
of the lower fall.

A few minutes' walk beyond this last bridge, as we approach the government housing area, the bridle path re-enters
from the right. Less than a quarter mile down this horse trail
a large bronze plaque on a granite boulder marks the site of
the log cabin that John Muir built and lived in for two years.
Continuing on our trail east, next to the cliffs, we start to
climb as we pass the government horse corral and maintenance
buildings. To the left a dim trail up an unforested section
leads to Sunnyside Ledge, about 300 feet up the cliff, one of
Muir's favorite observation points.

Continuing to climb, we pass behind the Visitor Center
and the Village area and reach some open areas with good
views of the Valley below. Going downhill, we cross a bridge
over Indian Canyon Creek, then pass Lewis Memorial Hospital
and come to the Church Bowl, where Sunday services are held.
The trail straight ahead goes to the Ahwahnee Hotel, the
stables, Indian Caves and Mirror Lake. We turn right (south)

and cross a large meadow on a blacktop trail near the houses of Curry Company employees. This trail crosses the road leading to the Village, then follows up the north bank of the Merced River for 200 yards, passing a section of Lower River Campground. Cross the wooden footbridge over the river and continue upstream on the west bank. After crossing another road, we are back on the trail between Camp Curry and Le Conte Memorial Lodge, and a quarter mile to the left is our starting point.

DAY HIKE #5

Yosemite Lodge to El Capitan Bridge via northside and southside trails (7½ miles)
3-4 hours

Most of this trail through the middle section of Yosemite Valley is well shaded, but there are enough open places to allow views of the Three Brothers, El Capitan, Cathedral Spires, Yosemite Falls and Sentinel Fall.

From Yosemite Lodge, proceed toward Yosemite Falls. Just beyond the Yosemite Falls parking lot, turn left at the comfort station and pick up the trail following close to the cliffs. Along here you will see the rocks on which, in the spring, rock-climbing classes practice techniques for getting up a vertical wall. The granite walls of Yosemite Valley are known throughout the world as among the best places to climb. A half mile west of our start is the beginning of the Yosemite Falls Trail. It is 3½ miles to the top of the falls, but

the nearly 3000-foot climb makes it the equivalent of about a 9-mile level walk.

Continuing west, we pass Sunnyside Camp, where numerous climbers and hikers camp. During spring and fall the campground is a mosaic of many small, colorful mountaineer's tents. About 100 yards beyond this camp, a trail leaves ours to cross the road and return to the Lodge area. We continue west another 150 yards, cross the road, and stroll downstream on the north bank of the Merced River, which glides silently as it meanders over the almost level Valley floor. A few minutes' walk along the river bank brings us to some pleasant open areas which offer views back to Yosemite Falls and across to small but distinctive Sentinel Fall. This fall is usually dry by early summer and Yosemite Falls sometimes disappears as early as late summer, but they are spectacular in the spring. Continuing westward, we pass the rocky triad called the Three Brothers, which are visible through the treetops on the right.

About 2.5 miles from the start we pass through the El Capitan picnic area, then cross an open meadow and arrive at the so-called Devil's Elbow. A side trail goes across the road here and continues westward down the canyon past El Capitan to the Pohono Bridge (see Day Hike #6). We stay on the river bank next to the road, and in one-third mile arrive at El Capitan Bridge, a good place from which to study the cliffs of El Capitan. You are looking directly at the "North America wall," so named because the darker rock on this wall is shaped surprisingly like a map of North America. The Florida Peninsula is missing, but perhaps that should be expected in the state of California. At times during the climbing season one can see climbers on their way up various routes on the vertical

rock wall. Across the Valley from El Capitan are the Cathedral Spires, and climbers can also be seen there occasionally.
Ascents of these spires in 1934 marked the beginning of
modern rock climbing in Yosemite.

Our trail, immediately after crossing the bridge, leads up
the Valley through a shady forest for a short half mile before
crossing the southside road, then after another quarter mile
joins the southside trail. Westward this trail leads to Bridalveil
Fall, Fern Spring and Pohono Bridge (see Day Hike #6). Turning left (east) through an open forest of ponderosa pine,
incense-cedar and black oak, we jump across several streams
that dry up by late summer. The trail is so far from the road
here that only the loudest vehicles can be heard. In the stillness, bird songs are delightful, gray squirrels with long, bushy
tails scamper about, and wildflowers and butterflies add their
color to the scene.

About two miles up the trail from the last road crossing, we
rockhop across seasonal Sentinel Creek and in springtime get
good views of its superb waterfall. The water first cascades
over the cliff top; then in numerous small falls it twists and
turns, disappearing and then leaping into view again in its
bouncing rush down the cliff to the talus slope below. Just
beyond Sentinel Creek is a road leading to the parking area
for the start of the Four Mile Trail to Glacier Point. Another
quarter mile brings us to some picnic tables where a sign marks
the site of Galen Clark's cabin. Clark was Guardian of
Yosemite Valley during the first twenty years that it was a
park, when it was governed by the State of California (1864-
1905). Here we turn left (north) and cross Swinging Bridge,
originally a cable bridge but now built on solid piers. Across

the bridge a blacktop path leads north, back to Yosemite
Lodge.

DAY HIKE #6

El Capitan Bridge to Pohono Bridge and Bridalveil Fall; loop trip via northside and southside trails (6½ miles) 3-4 hours

From the north end of El Capitan Bridge, this pleasant walk
leads upstream along the north bank of the Merced River.
Soon we come to the Devil's Elbow scenic area, where we turn
left (north) across the road, then left again (west), and proceed down the Valley toward El Capitan on a little-used trail.
Our route joins a closed road which was the original road up
the Valley from the Big Oak Flat and the Coulterville roads,
then climbs over a low hill, the remains of a recessional moraine left by the last glacier. On the west side of this moraine
is an open area near the nose of El Capitan, and when there
are climbers on the cliff, this is a good place to watch them.

As we approach the main northside road, we leave the old
roadway and turn right (northwest) onto a trail that is sometimes hard to follow. Looking up to the north, one can get
occasional glimpses of Ribbon Fall, the highest single water
drop in North America. Just beyond the crossing of Ribbon
Creek is a junction with the old Big Oak Flat Road. This
route was built as a toll road but was bought by the state and
used until the 1930s, when it was wiped out by numerous
rock slides. A new road down from Crane Flat was then

constructed through tunnels. The old route was a controlled
one-way road. Traffic downhill started on the even hours and
uphill on the odd, so if you were ten minutes late you had to
wait an hour and fifty minutes to travel over this section.

Our route turns left (south) and goes down the old road to
a locked gate, where it turns right and continues west again.
We climb over two old moraines, and from near the top of the
second one we can see the brink of delightful Bridalveil Fall.
The trail meets the road at Pohono Bridge, and across the
bridge it curves left (east). About 150 yards up the road is
lovely Fern Spring, but its water may be polluted. However,
you can tank up at trailside Moss Spring not far beyond. The
forest here is a great mixture of ponderosa pines, sugar pines,
incense-cedars, black oaks, live oaks, Douglas-firs and some
large dogwoods. Bracken ferns and the common horsetail cover
the forest floor, and in the spring yellow and blue violets peek
up at the traveler as they poke above the mat of oak leaves and
pine needles.

The next meadow is a historical site, for it was here that
John Muir sat beside a campfire with President Theodore
Roosevelt and discussed the need to preserve the priceless
remnants of America's wilderness. The trail may be indistinct
here but it does not cross the road. Rather, it swings left
toward the river on the far side of the meadow.

We soon come to several branches of Bridalveil Creek, and
there are usually footlogs for crossing. During spring runoffs,
when the crossings are difficult, cross on the highway bridge
nearby. A quarter mile farther the trail crosses the southside
road and gets lost in a maze of paths through a picnic area.
The solution is to walk toward the cliffs to an old road. Here

the route turns left (east), but first one should turn right
(west) for a closer approach to the base of descriptively named
Bridalveil Fall. Continuing east, we climb the talus slope at
the foot of Cathedral Rocks. At the crest of this climb there
are marvelous views across the canyon to Ribbon Fall and the
southwest face of El Capitan. Another mile brings us to a
trail leading left (north), which returns us to our starting point
at El Capitan Bridge.

DAY HIKE #7

Happy Isles to Sierra Point (1½ miles, 4 eq. miles, round trip)
2-3 hours

This comparatively little-used trail leads to a lookout with
a stupendous view, where you can see Nevada Fall, Vernal Fall,
Illilouette Fall and Upper and Lower Yosemite Falls. Due to
the steepness of the climb (about 800 feet elevation in about
a half mile), it is fairly strenuous.

From Happy Isles a blacktop footpath, the start of the
John Muir Trail, climbs gradually, winding among large blocks
of granite talus which have fallen from the cliffs above. Wel-
come shade is provided by the live oaks, maples, incense-cedars
and Douglas-firs. About 200 yards up the path at an unmarked junction, a trail to the right leads back to several foot-
bridges that link the Happy Isles. The dim trail to the left is
our trail to Sierra Point. A few yards beyond this junction is a
good spring which has deliciously cool water.

The first part of the Sierra Point trail is fairly steep, in places so steep that granite blocks have been emplaced as steps. California laurels, or bay trees, grow profusely on this slope, and on a warm day the hiker's nostrils are full of their pungent odor. After a few switchbacks, the trail comes close to some nearly bare granite cliffs, scraped clean by the Merced Glacier, which came down the canyon below. Since the glacier melted, lichens and mosses have begun to grow on the rock, as have a few flowers and even a small tree or two.

About halfway up, just before you reach a steel cable, is an open viewpoint where you can look down on the forested floor of the Valley below. Across the Valley are Upper and Lower Yosemite Falls, breathtaking during the spring runoff. Off to the right are the Royal Arches and Washington Column, with North Dome above them and Basket Dome farther right. Toward the left are the cliffs of Glacier Point, rising vertically from the Glacier Point apron.

The trail now climbs steeply and a steel cable helps one negotiate about eight feet of rock, but this route is not dangerous if one is careful and takes his time. This is a good section of trail on which to practice the mountaineer's rest step, a method of traveling on steep grades and in high elevations. The hiker rests at each step, rather than rushing a short distance and then stopping, completely out of breath. Just as your forward foot touches the ground, lock your back knee, keeping your weight on the rear foot and using the forward foot for balance only. Pause for anywhere from a fraction of a second to several seconds, depending on the terrain and your condition. Your breathing rate will determine the length of pause. One need never walk so fast that he is too out of breath to carry on a conversation. Using the rest step, one can keep going for hours with only occasional stops to admire the view or take a picture.

After a short but steep quarter mile, we reach the top of the climb and traverse on an almost level trail around some rocky cliffs. In the spring and early summer one can look across the canyon here to spy a small stream leaping and bounding down the cliffs in a joyous descent from Glacier Point to the Merced River below. Then, around the first bend, Illilouette Fall comes into view, with a cloud of mist at its feet and the water cascading down the steep, narrow canyon below. Finally we arrive at Sierra Point. To the left we see Vernal and Nevada falls. Illilouette Fall is straight ahead and slightly higher, and to the right are Upper and Lower Yosemite Falls. Seeing five world-famous waterfalls from this one point is a worthwhile reward for the energy expended.

In retracing your steps to the John Muir Trail, be extremely careful to stay on the trail, as it is fairly easy to miss a switch-back when going down. If you should find yourself off-trail, retrace your steps at once. Although it may look easy going as far as you can see, there are nearly vertical cliffs below almost all the trail.

DAY HIKE #8

Old Big Oak Flat Road to new Big Oak Flat Road
(4 miles; 6 eq. miles in the opposite direction)
2 hours down; 3 hours up

This hike is at lower elevations, making it a good spring or fall walk, and combining it with Day Hike #9 makes a good all-day hike. In spring and early summer the trail is lush with wildflower gardens and fern glens. Some of the exciting flowers you can expect to see are azalea, dogwood, tiger lily, lupine, pussy paws, mariposa lily, snow plant and pine drops.

On the Tioga Road, 3.6 miles east of the Crane Flat Road junction, a road goes south at a sign reading *Tamarack Flat Campground 3*. This road, a portion of the old Big Oak Flat Road, continues about 2.5 miles beyond the campground, ending at Cascade Creek. The start of the trail is 150 yards back uphill from the end of the road. Immediately the trail crosses an unnamed tributary of Cascade Creek, where, if you are fortunate, you may see one of the water ouzels that make this stream their home.

Beyond the stream, the trail is almost level through an open forest of incense-cedar, ponderosa and sugar pine, and white fir, with occasional red-barked manzanita shrubs growing underneath. As the trail contours along a steep hillside, the open forest allows a good view across Merced canyon to Turtleback Dome. Then we descend gently to moderately, kicking some large sugar-pine cones out of the way, to cross a trickling stream. This stream is usually dry by midsummer, but earlier its banks are a beautiful garden of azaleas. We continue down, rockhop across Tamarack Creek, and climb a quarter mile up the other side before rounding a ridge. The trail then descends again, moderately, crossing several more small, trickling streams, each with its own miniature wild-flower garden in early season.

After an easy crossing of Wildcat Creek, you ascend gently, then make an almost level contour before the last moderate switchbacking descent to the new Big Oak Flat Road. On this descent Big Meadow appears below, nestled among the forested mountain slopes. You may see tracks of bears and coyotes on the trail, or even one of these wild creatures itself. The bright green growth decorating the trunks and branches of the trees on this hillside is not a moss, as it is often called, but staghorn lichen, a complicated plant which is a partnership of fungi and algae. This easy, delightful walk ends on the new Big Oak Flat Road at its junction with the Foresta-Big Meadow road.

DAY HIKE #9

Old Big Oak Flat Road to Yosemite Valley
(5 miles; 9 eq. miles in the opposite direction)
3 hours down; 5 hours up

This historical route, once a primary wagon road into the Valley, is now impassable to vehicles and horses, and is used only by an occasional hiker. The roadend trailhead is at the crossing of Cascade Creek (see Day Hike #8). There is only limited parking here (3-4 cars) and no camping. The blacktop "trail" begins with a steady, gentle descent through a fairly dense forest of sugar and ponderosa pine, incense-cedar and white fir, with chinquapin and manzanita underneath. In spring and early summer, Cascade Creek can be heard making its musical way down the canyon on the right.

About a half mile down the old road is a junction with the El Capitan Trail, a much longer and more strenuous route to the Valley (Day Hike #10). Another half mile down, the road-

trail emerges into an open area with excellent views across the
Valley to Turtleback Dome and Inspiration Point and down
the Merced Gorge. Across the Valley one can see the highway
where it enters the Wawona Tunnel; above it are Inspiration
Point and sections of the old Wawona Road. Down to the
right, just off the Valley floor, is distinctive Pulpit Rock and
behind us, to the north, are neck-bending views of Fireplace
Bluffs.

The steadily descending trail crosses several alder-clad
streams with cool, refreshing water. At Fireplace Creek the
old road has been washed away, but the hiker should have no
trouble picking his way up and around any of the breaks in the
roadway. On this descent evergreens give way to deciduous
trees, and one soon sees black oaks, golden oaks and an occasional rare California torreya. Perhaps your nose will tell
you before your eyes do that you are passing California bay
trees, and early-season hikers will detect the fragrance of the
showy western azalea long before they see it. Colorful clumps
of lupine, paintbrush, thistle and penstemon provide relief on
the otherwise dry, brushy slopes. Views of the opposite Valley
wall are abundant, but nowhere on this walk are they better
than at Rainbow View Point.

Just below this viewpoint the trail (the road is seen only
occasionally now) disappears under an immense rockslide. A
short way out onto this rockslide, the old road switchbacked;
if it is difficult to stay on the route, just look down and
see portions of the old road over 100 feet below. Be very
careful boulder-hopping over these rocks, as some rocks may
be unstable. The rocks of these slides, what geologists call
diorites, are the oldest rocks in Yosemite Valley. At a point

directly across from Bridalveil Creek, one may inspect the glacially created hanging valley that makes up the drainage of Bridalveil Creek. The view of Yosemite Valley from here is framed by El Capitan on the left and Cathedral Rocks on the right. The meadow below Bridalveil Fall is where John Muir and President Teddy Roosevelt camped one night in 1903, when Muir urged the President to work for preservation of the priceless remnants of America's wilderness.

As our trail re-enters coniferous forest cover, Ribbon Fall comes into view on the near side of the Valley. From here, incense-cedars and ponderosa pines shade the trail as it comes within hearing of Ribbon Creek, then joins a maintenance road that takes us to the main road on the north side of the Valley.

DAY HIKE #10

Old Big Oak Flat Road to Yosemite Valley via the El Capitan Trail
(17 miles; 22 eq. miles; 25 eq. miles in the opposite direction)
10 hours

This extremely long and strenuous hike should be attempted only by people in excellent physical condition who have taken other long hikes recently. The views from this trail are stupendous, perhaps not equaled from any other trail in the Park. There are several stream crossings until midsummer, but in late summer Ribbon and Yosemite creeks are the only streams that can be relied on for water, and a canteen is in order then.

This route starts on the old Big Oak Flat Road 2.5 miles
below Tamarack Flat campground. At the trailhead there is
only limited parking (3-4 cars) and no camping. The old road
crosses Cascade Creek on a substantial bridge and continues
down a half mile to a junction with the El Capitan Trail on the
left, where a sign reads *El Capitan 5.5, Eagle Peak 7.9,
Yosemite Valley 13.3.* Adjusting for elevation gain, these
distances in eq. miles become: El Capitan 9.5, Eagle Peak 12,
Yosemite Valley 19.5. A shorter route to the Valley continues
down the old roadway (see Day Hike #9). Leaving the blacktop we climb moderately through a forest of ponderosa,
Jeffrey and sugar pine and white fir, where the ground is almost covered with a mixture of their cones. About a mile up-
trail we climb a granite slope that is bare except for a few isolated Jeffrey pines which somehow find enough sustenance in
the meager fingers of sand and gravel that lace this otherwise
massive rock.

We continue our steady climb along a broad, open ridge, in
one section pushing through a waist-high "forest" of huckle-
berry oaks. At Ribbon Creek one may take a well-earned rest
and enjoy the almost absolute silence, interrupted only by an
occasional bird song, accompanied by strains of water music
from the stream.

Beyond this creek we continue an undulating climb and
soon get glimpses of the great El Capitan ahead. Topping El
Capitan ridge we come to a trail junction marked only by a
small pile of rocks. From here a spur trail actually *descends*
to the summit of this world-renowned granite monolith. On
the summit is a head-high monument of rocks and a register
box. At this point the hiker can boast that he has climbed El

Capitan (no need to elaborate that it was from the back side). The views to the east and south are unrestricted. All the famous points of the Valley and its south rim are easy to identify. The whole of the Clark Range is beyond. Even the first glacier found in the Sierra, by John Muir, is visible on the north side of Merced Peak. In several places rock walls have been built to protect campers from the wind, but wood is scarce and there is no water.

Continuing our hike, we return to the unmarked trail junction, take the right (east) fork and contour along the ridge that extends north from El Capitan. A short mile farther on, we cross a trickle of water that may still be running past mid-summer, then descend about 200 feet to Eagle Creek, which is dry soon after the snow melts on Eagle Peak. We climb this usually dry stream bed to a slight saddle just north of Eagle Peak. Beyond this low saddle, one descends about 300 yards to a junction with a trail going right (south). A sign here reads *Eagle Peak 0.3.* This trail climbs fairly steeply, and it must be longer than the signed 0.3 to this peak, the highest of the Three Brothers, so one should go slowly in the rarefied air. At the summit one finds a register box, and unlimited views in almost all directions. The statement that many hikers have written in the register, "The views from here are fantastic," is true. One looks directly down on Leidig Meadow, and all the Valley floor is laid out like a full-scale map. Across the Valley, Sentinel Dome is very evident, and down to its left is Glacier Point. To the west is the rounded summit of El Capitan. South beyond the Valley rim is Horse Ridge, and in the southeast are all the peaks of the Clark Range. Farther left is Half Dome and directly over its summit is Mt. Florence,

named for the first white baby born in Yosemite Valley. Up
to the left of Half Dome is Clouds Rest, then Cathedral Peak
and the other peaks of the Tuolumne Meadows region. Northeast on the skyline is distinctive Mt. Conness, and northward
Mt. Hoffmann dominates the view. Reluctantly we leave this
magnificent high place and retrace our steps to the main trail.

The descent from the trail junction to Yosemite Creek is
a delightful walk through a forest that varies from dense to
open. In the spring and summer many colorful wildflowers
cheer us on as perhaps by now a tired feeling begins to set in.
When Eagle Peak Creek is flowing in the spring and early summer, we jump across it near its head and then rockhop across
it just before reaching the Yosemite Creek Trail. There is always some water in Yosemite Creek about a quarter mile up
this trail. At this junction we turn south, downhill. Yosemite
Creek itself is over a rock ridge to the east. About a half mile
down the trail we arrive at another junction, from where a
trail east goes to the brink of Yosemite Falls, Yosemite Point
and North Dome. (For a description of this trail and the trail
up Yosemite Creek to the Tioga Road, see the High Sierra
Hiking Guide to *Hetch Hetchy*.)

From this junction our trail makes a long series of switchbacks down the height of Upper Yosemite Fall, but the fall is
not seen until we are nearly at its base. Even then we get only
glimpses through the trees, but when the flow is full, the fall is
awe-inspiring, and it is possible to become drenched by the
wind-swept spray. At other times there may be just a fine
mist.

Near the base of the upper fall the trail becomes level, then
starts climbing as it turns a corner westward. We have to shift

back to our climbing muscles for a long quarter mile as we pass a trickle of cool water and then continue to climb across an avalanche area where a rock fall in 1973 wiped out a part of the trail below Columbia Rock and closed it for a few weeks. Beyond this devastated area are more switchbacks down a very sandy trail—well shaded, however, by oaks and bay trees—to trail's end at Sunnyside Camp. There is a parking lot next to the service station here, and across the road at Yosemite Lodge is a shuttlebus stop.

DAY HIKE #11

Glacier Point to Yosemite Valley via the Four Mile Trail (4½ miles; 10 eq. miles in the opposite direction) 2 hours down; 4 hours up

This day hike has been a historical favorite of Valley visitors for over 100 years because of its panoramic views of the Valley. Built in 1871 by J. McCauley, it was initially a toll trail, and was open to the hearty for a fee of $1.

Beginning at Glacier Point the trail is intermittently well-worn duff, asphalt and dust. Near the Point, the forest is dense with Jeffrey and sugar pines mixed with red and white firs and occasional Douglas-firs. The views are at first restricted, but soon North and Basket domes come into sight. After descending gently to a small stream, our path contours out to the brink of the Valley to the first of the trail's famous viewpoints.

The trail then switchbacks down over an exposed granite

slope, where the ground cover is mostly manzanita, chinquapin and *Ceanothus*. This abrupt descent levels off briefly at Union Point. Some accounts have it that this point was the site of the trail builder's private summer home—a wood wigwam that sported an American flag at its apex. In any event, the Union Point view area, bounded by iron-pipe railings, commands one of the finest views of Yosemite Valley and of nearby Agassiz Columns. Each landmark is distinct, and many of the Valley waterfalls are in view. In 1973 there was a good water fountain 30 yards up-trail from the side trail that leads to the overlook.

From Union Point, the trail descends steeply, clinging to the near-vertical granite facade. Hikers will find the matrix rock walls on the uphill sides of this section of the trail a fascinating study in trail workmanship. Most of the trees found at Union Point and along the trail below are of the broadleaved variety, including oak and mountain laurel. With the towering eminence of Sentinel Rock dominating the near wall, the trail descends to the ford of tumbling Sentinel Creek. After the ford, the trail continues its steady descent, and some 200 feet above the Valley floor, winds through the shade of Douglas-firs and ponderosa pines. One does not encounter the incense-cedar until actually on the Valley floor, where the trail ends at a parking loop 1.25 miles from Yosemite Village.

> "To me, the difference between meditation and prayer is this: If your mind is ever to become still, you will find that the dialogue in your mind has stopped."
>
> Joan Baez, *Daybreak*

DAY HIKE #12

Glacier Point to Wawona Tunnel via the Pohono Trail
(13 miles; 16 eq. miles; 21 eq. miles in the opposite direction)
8 hours westbound; 10 hours eastbound

Until midsummer this is a superb wildflower trail. Among
those you may expect to see are snow plant, pussy paws,
larkspur, Mariposa lily, shooting star, yellow monkey flower,
Indian paintbrush, groundsel, azalea, red columbine, pennyroyal, thimbleberry and many ferns. In order to enjoy a hike
this long, one must be in good physical condition. Otherwise
the trip can be made into two hikes by using the McGurk
Meadow lateral (Lateral Trail #2), or it could be made as an
overnight backpack trip by using the Bridalveil Creek campsites.

Starting from a large wooden sign above the parking lot at
Glacier Point, the Pohono Trail goes uphill behind the sign,
crosses the road, and at a fork goes right (the left fork goes to
a ranger's cabin). Our trail climbs around and above this cabin
and crosses a road leading to some water tanks. We continue
climbing, skirt Sentinel Dome on our left, and pass a short
half-mile lateral to the top of this once extremely popular
dome. Thousands of people visited it each year when they
could drive to within 100 feet of the summit. Now that the
short approach road is closed, only hundreds do so. It is well
worth the short side jaunt to look at this massive, ice-resistant
granite, to imagine when the top protruded only about 100
feet above the surface of the Yosemite glacier, and to enjoy
the unlimited views in all directions. Retracing our steps to

the Pohono Trail, we continue around Sentinel Dome, jump across Sentinel Creek, and then ascend through lodgepole, Jeffrey and silver pine mixed with fir. About one mile beyond the stream, a side trail branches left to the Glacier Point Road. Our trail then descends on sand past the deeply cleft rocks called The Fissures and reaches a trail junction about 100 yards from a breathtaking exposure of overhanging Taft Point.

From the junction, the trail then descends steadily, first across a glaciated slope, and finally into a dense red-fir forest. The damp sections along this trail are havens for many kinds of colorful wildflowers. Our duff trail descends to the lodgepole-pine-clad banks of Bridalveil Creek, and crosses on a well-built bridge near some good campsites. Many of the pines here are "ghost" snags, the work of the needle-miner insect. Beyond the bridge, the trail ascends gently over sand, and passes the McGurk Meadow Trail (see Lateral Trail #2) branching left to the Glacier Point Road.

The terrain undulates as the trail crosses tributaries of Bridalveil Creek, and the forest cover now shows the inclusion of sugar pine amid the predominant red and white firs. This section of trail brings us to Dewey Point, from where there are excellent views across the Valley to El Capitan and Ribbon Fall, and to the Clark Range in the east. From this point the trail descends moderately to Crocker Point, then more steeply to Stanford Point, where tired travelers can take a rest stop in the shade of Douglas-firs. From Stanford Point the trail ascends steadily around old Inspiration Point (no trail to it) to the ford of Meadow Brook. There are usually logs to help in crossing. Then, topping an easy rise, we descend to rockhop across Artist Creek.

The descent from this point is moderate-to-steep over a dusty surface where deciduous trees grow among the firs. The dry, dusty trail veers north and then east along the old Wawona Road, affording fine views up Yosemite Valley as it finally drops to the parking area at the east end of the Wawona Tunnel.

DAY HIKE #13

Glacier Point to Happy Isles via Panorama Trail and Mist Trail (8 miles; 9 eq. miles; 15 eq. miles in the opposite direction) 4 hours down; 7 hours up

This trail is an excellent foot route from Glacier Point to the Valley. The foot traveler has the advantage over the mounted traveler of being able to negotiate the Mist Trail.

The view from Glacier Point—or from Washburn Point—includes Nevada Fall, Vernal Fall, Half Dome, Mt. Starr King and the High Sierra, and the high-mountain beauty of these views is among the finest scenery in the world. In addition, on a clear day (and it is clearer in the morning), one can look across the vast chasm of the Merced River and with the aid of binoculars see hikers on the summit of Half Dome.

This trail begins at a large wooden sign above the parking lot at Glacier Point. Going left (east) from the sign, we swing south and descend into Illilouette Gorge, where we can see the work of avalanches that have thundered down from the heights, carrying rocks, trees and soil across the trail. Across Illilouette Gorge, one can see a cliff from which a large rock face fell in the winter of 1968-69. This major act of erosion struck the area just below a viewpoint situated on the switchbacks that climb the east canyon wall from Illilouette Creek.

At the junction with the Buena Vista Trail, our route turns left (east) and begins a switchbacking descent of 560 feet to Illilouette Creek. About one-third mile before the creek bridge is a chasm viewpoint just off the trail behind a small fence. From here there is a striking view almost directly down to 370-foot Illilouette Fall. Beyond the bridge over the creek, the trail rises steeply for 400 feet and then skirts Panorama Cliff. As we climb higher, views expand greatly. The Valley floor is spread out below, and across the canyon the immense back of Half Dome dominates the scene. At one point this granite wall is bracketed by Mt. Hoffmann on the left and Clouds Rest on the right, with Liberty Cap at its base. (Note that Half Dome has its "Royal Arches" also.)

To reach the top of Nevada Fall, we make a 600-foot descent past the junction with the trail shown on the topo map as the Mono Meadow Trail and then join the John Muir Trail coming up from the Valley, on which we turn right (east) and continue to the bridge just above Nevada Fall.

From the lip of Nevada Fall, we see Liberty Cap on the right, Glacier Point high ahead, and, below, the Merced River descending in cascades and pools, and finally disappearing over Vernal Fall.

Nevada Fall drops 594 feet in a fantastic display of water, striking granite ledges and ricocheting out as plumes of spray. Other falls in Yosemite drop greater distances, but none has as much water as Nevada, whose thunderous roar can be heard for miles.

The traveler may decide to conclude his hike via the relatively gentle descent along the horse trail (part of the John Muir Trail) to the Valley, which requires a short retracing of steps to the last junction. The more spectacular route, however, is via the Mist Trail. As this route is spectacular, it is also somewhat difficult, due to its many hewn-rock steps. Rubber or composition soles, preferably with lugs, are a must on this slippery trail.

In 1973 part of the upper portion of this route was severely damaged by rock slides, and until the trail is repaired, extreme caution is required to rockhop down over the sometimes unstable granite blocks, and the trail may be closed during periods of reconstruction.

Beginning one-quarter mile northeast of the top of Nevada Fall, progress is easily measured in relation to Nevada Fall, since the trail at one point comes near the base of the fall. At this point the immense power of the fall makes itself known. This route imposes an unforgettable humility on all who tread it. Leaving the road of the fall behind, we climb gently a short distance before descending to cross a good bridge over the Merced River. From the bridge one can see the water downstream spread out and glide or cascade—depending on the volume—over a smooth granite section of riverbed. From this gliding cascade, called the Silver Apron, the river plunges with bubbly froth into placid Emerald Pool. This quiet section of the river evokes a feeling of calm, but just a minute away the same water is catapulted with a roar into the misty chasm below Vernal Fall. The apparent calm of the water in the pools above the fall should *not* be interpreted to mean safe swimming! The rocks are slippery and the water has great force.

Do not enter the water for *any* reason above the fall.

Climbing a short distance away from the fall, the route descends steeply, sometimes on granite steps, into the misty depths below. It is on this section that the trail's name gains meaning, for until late summer one emerges from a cloud of mist 400 feet lower with clothing damp and ears ringing with the sound of crashing water.

About 200 yards before reaching Vernal Fall bridge the Mist Trail joins the John Muir Trail on its descent to Happy Isles and the Valley floor.

DAY HIKE #14

Bridalveil Campground to Wawona via the Alder Creek Trail (13 miles; 19 eq. miles in the opposite direction) 6 hours southbound and 9 hours northbound

This long route, all downhill, is very little used. The terrain and scenery vary from lush, boggy meadows to open, warm, dry hillsides. Starting at a telephone booth at the Bridalveil Campground entrance, this trail proceeds west on a portion of the old Glacier Point Road. Less than half a mile down this old roadway, we cross flower-filled Peregoy Meadow and come to a trail junction. The roadway continues straight ahead and the trail going right (north) crosses the Glacier Point Road and passes through McGurk Meadow to meet the Pohono Trail (see Lateral Trail #2). Our trail goes left (south) and climbs gently through a continuous garden of wildflowers growing under a forest of lodgepole pines. About a mile farther we cross

Westfall Meadows, quite wet and boggy. By staying on the foot trail rather than the horse trail, one may possibly avoid wet feet.

Beyond the meadow the rejoined trails climb more steeply for a short distance, then begin to descend into the Alder Creek drainage. We cross a small tributary stream, drink of the refreshing water, and notice the perfection of the wild geraniums blooming here in season. Then descending to the Deer Camp road, we follow it westward. This road, now used as a fire road by the Park Service, was built as a railroad to haul logs from a private holding within the Park to the west end of Henness Ridge, where the logs were lowered on a cable-incline road to El Portal.

After a half mile our route turns left (south) off the roadway and continues, keeping left at two unmarked trail forks. There are a number of old roads and trails in this area, built when there were private land holdings around here. Beyond several flowering meadows there is a signed junction where a trail going left leads to Deer Camp and to the Buck Camp Trail (see Lateral Trail #1). We turn right, down Alder Creek, and soon cross it on good footlogs. A short distance downstream is a small campsite, and pan-sized trout can be seen in the stream.

Descending moderately along this beautifully forested, flower-bordered trail, we come again to an old railroad grade, which we follow for a couple of miles. The rails are gone, but some of the ties are still left, along with cables and other equipment. Just beyond Alder Creek Fall where a lovely, cool, spring-fed stream invites a stop, there is an excellent place for the camera buff to get an intimate picture of a beautiful little waterfall. The trail is rather overgrown with

brush for a short distance, but when it leaves the railroad
right-of-way it enters a parklike grove of immense sugar pines.
The forest floor is almost totally covered with their large
cones. The reddish-brown spiked plants growing here about
knee-high, called pine drops, do not manufacture their own
food by photosynthesis but exist on decaying vegetation.
Beyond several small streams that are usually dry by midsummer is another trail junction, where the trail to the right
(west) goes 0.7 mile to a distinctive horseshoe bend in the
Wawona highway. Our trail descends moderately over south-
west-facing slopes where mountain mahogany, with its curled,
feathery catkins, grows alongside other plants that like the
warmer, drier hillsides. In several places the trail is deeply
eroded; little-used trails, such as this one, do not get as much
maintenance as the popular ones. The open hillsides offer
good views across the canyon of the South Fork of the Merced
River to the forested ridge beyond. Ahead are the timbered
ridges of the Mariposa Grove, and to the east is Wawona Dome.
Near Wawona a spur trail goes right to descend to a service
road, and our main trail continues over to Chilnualna Road,
ending just above the ranger station.

DAY HIKE #15

Mariposa Grove to Wawona
(6 miles; 9 eq. miles in the opposite direction)
3 hours down; 4 hours up

There are several miles of trails in and around the Mariposa
Grove itself, and one could enjoy a full day or more walking

under these incredibly old giants. A free map of the trails is available at the parking lot, and free open-air trams make stops at points of interest. One can ride to the fallen Tunnel Tree, a high point in the grove, and walk back downhill from there. From the fallen Tunnel Tree an easy half-mile climb to Wawona Point is small payment for the extensive views from there. Looking eastward up the South Fork of the Merced River, one can see Gale and Sing peaks and the other mountains that form the southeast boundary of the Park. To the north is Wawona Dome and the forested country beyond. Northwestward are the meadows of Wawona and the lower canyon of the South Fork. From this high point there are several trails down to the museum, which should be visited, and to the defunct Big Trees Lodge. One can learn much about the Sequoias from a self-guiding loop trail that starts at the museum.

The hike to Wawona can be started from the parking lot, the Grizzly Giant, or the Big Trees Lodge. Proceed to the trail junction west of the grove, from where it is 5 downhill miles to the hotel and store at Wawona. When leaving the grove we see that the giant sequoias are not the only big trees here: some ponderosa pines and sugar pines have also attained immense dimensions.

We descend moderately down a few switchbacks along a well-shaded trail. About a mile from the last junction we cross a stream that is boisterous during the runoff season and flows well past midsummer. Beyond, a controlled burn area is evidence of a new Park Service policy. Periodic fire was natural in the forest before the white man came, but his penchant for putting out fires has prevented many trees and

plants from reseeding themselves because they need bare
mineral soil to propagate. Midway along the route we come
close to the Wawona highway; then, as we veer away, the trail
forks. The unmarked right (east) fork leads to a summer camp
near the upper end of the South Wawona road. Our unmarked
left (west) fork passes several more unmarked junctions where
the main route is quite evident. Upon reaching the rear of the
Wawona Hotel, we continue to the right (northeast) to skirt
the hotel complex and reach the South Wawona road just
above the parking lot near the Pioneer Village and the store.

DAY HIKE #16

Wawona Road to the South Fork of the Merced River
(4 miles down; 7 eq. miles in the opposite direction)
2 hours down; 3 hours up

This trail, not shown on the topo map, is at elevations
suitable for a spring or fall hike. The angler may find fishing
good in both the river and the creek. The trail starts at a long,
wide shoulder on the Wawona Road, about 0.1 mile up the
road from the crossing of Alder Creek and 7.4 miles from
Chinquapin Ranger Station. A sign just over the shoulder
(not visible from the road) reads *Alder Creek Trail–weapons
and pets prohibited.*

The trail descends gently into a stream bed that is dry most
of the year, then joins a section of the old Wawona Road,
which it follows for a short distance. The open forest here is
composed mainly of large ponderosa pines, incense-cedars and

black oaks, and the forest floor is covered with a thick carpet of aromatic kit-kit-dizze. Leaving the roadway, our trail contours high along the canyon wall, then descends gently for about a mile to the Park border.

Continuing down into Sierra National Forest for a half mile, we arrive at an unnamed intermittent stream. This stream usually flows past midsummer, and there are extensive campsites here. Another mile down is Bishop Creek, a good flowing stream even in the fall, and here also is a good campsite.

Beyond Bishop Creek the trail traverses south-facing slopes, and the vegetation changes abruptly to plants that like a warmer climate, including digger pine, buckeye, poison oak and mountain mahogany.

The trail descends more steeply now, and as we approach the bottom of the canyon, we pass a trail going right (west) down the canyon. In 1973 there was no marker at this junction but only a white 4-by-4 post lying on the ground. Taking the left fork at this junction and proceeding about 200 yards downhill brings us to another crossing of Bishop Creek, just above its mouth at the South Fork of the Merced River.

Across the creek is a cabin, and a trail goes up around a small corral and leads to the river. About 100 yards upstream is a good campsite near clear pools with trout 8-12″ long.

"Is it worth living in L.A. smog for 50 weeks in order to spend two weeks in Yosemite valley which in the summer may be even more crowded than L.A. and twice as smoggy?"
Dr. Paul Ehrlich

BACKPACK TRAIL #1

Bridalveil Campground to Glacier Point via Royal Arch Lake
(28½ miles; 36 eq. miles)

This long and scenic route mostly follows little-used trails. Until late summer the trailside is almost one continous flower garden, and one can expect to see over 25 different varieties, from low-growing pussy paws and violets to head-high corn lilies and tiger lilies. The trip requires a short car shuttle.

The trail starts from the southeast end of Bridalveil Campground, where parking space is limited. Should it be full, the trip can be started from a large parking area about a mile east on the Glacier Point Road. From there, use the Ostrander Lake Trail (Backpack Trail #3) and the quarter-mile lateral to our trail. Starting from the Bridalveil Campground our trail, the Buck Camp Trail, is almost level as it ascends the west bank of Bridalveil Creek. About 1.8 miles up this trail is a junction with a short lateral to the Ostrander Lake Trail. Beyond this junction, our trail leaves Bridalveil Creek and ascends along a tributary stream. Just before the crossing of this stream there is a campsite, and after it an unsigned trail junction with another lateral to the Ostrander Lake Trail.

Continuing the gentle climb for another mile, the trail crosses three small streams, then ascends more steeply to a broad ridge. As we keep to the top of this ridge for a short distance, the sparse forest allows views down into the canyon of the South Fork of the Merced River. Then, leaving the ridgetop to contour along its southwest side we wade through waist-high ferns, gooseberries and currant bushes. Beyond an aspen grove the trail crosses a boggy but beautifully flowered meadow and passes the Deer Camp Trail (Lateral Trail #1). Topping a low divide, our trail descends gently down the headwaters of a Chilnualna Creek tributary, past Turner Meadows, named for a pioneer who used the extensive meadows for summer pasturage. A pile of rocks marks the fireplace of Bill Turner's cabin, and there is a small campsite near the stream close by. About a mile farther, at a stream crossing not shown on the topo map, is a packer campsite. A short distance beyond it, a trail goes right (southwest) to Wawona, and 0.8 mile farther on another one goes left (east) to Chilnualna Lakes. (Backpack Trail #2 describes these routes.)

We rockhop across Chilnualna Creek and climb moderately up the ridge between it and a tributary coming out of Grouse Lake. Beyond the ridge, the trail from Wawona (Backpack Trail #2) meets ours, and the conjoined route rises eastward into a predominantly lodgepole-pine forest. Flower gardens of shooting star, corn lily, yarrow, lupine, aster, Indian paintbrush and pennyroyal—among others—are still continuous.

The trail continues its moderate climb past Grouse and Crescent lakes. Both lakes are reedy, but they can provide a catch of trout for the expert or lucky fisherman, and there are good campsites at both. Beyond Crescent Lake we descend a mile to Johnson Lake, skirt the north side of the lake past several good campsites, and wade across the inlet stream. Beyond the ford we climb again to a trail junction, where we leave the Buck Camp Trail. (For a description of the trails east of here see the High Sierra Hiking Guide to *Merced Peak*.)

About a half mile north on the Buena Vista Trail, we come to dramatic Royal Arch Lake. Its name derives from the black

Royal Arch Lake and catch

streaks that rainbow across the steep granite cliffs that domi-
nate the eastern side of the lake bowl. The streaks are dark
lichens, growing on the nearly white granite. This lake is a
popular camping spot, with good campsites. There are good-
sized trout also, but a short, easy, cross-country walk west
over a ridge takes one to Minnow Lake, which is less often
fished. Leaving Royal Arch Lake we climb the Buena Vista
Crest and reach the highest point on this trip. Nearby to the
southwest is Buena Vista Peak, the highest point in the
Yosemite quadrangle; the peak is easily climbed from either
the north or the south side.

Just below Buena Vista Lake (good campsites) a trail goes
west to the Chilnualna Lakes and on to Wawona (see Backpack
Trail #2). From this junction there are good views northward
to Mt. Starr King and Half Dome, and on a clear day Mt.
Hoffmann can be seen on the skyline. Our route descends to
Buena Vista Creek, easily crosses and recrosses it, and then
fords the outlet stream of Hart Lakes. One can go cross-
country up this stream to Hart and Ostrander lakes (see Backpack Trail #3). Almost immediately we climb over a spur that
extends northward from Horse Ridge and one can also go cross-
country up this spur to Hart Lakes. The descent from this
ridge passes a dim trail to Edson Lake and enters a fairly dense
lodgepole-pine forest, with many dead snags, killed by the
needle-miner moth. Just before the outlet stream of Edson
Lake is a good campsite, and then the trail loops eastward out
of *Yosemite* quad for about a mile.

In this mile we come close to the confluence of Buena Vista
and Illilouette creeks, and then veer away from the latter as we
follow its canyon downstream. We jump across several small

tributaries, and then as we approach Illilouette Creek again we pass the trail coming down from Mono Meadow (Backpack Trail #5). There are several good campsites along both sides of the stream nearby. Because these campsites are much used, there are bears here that have learned that humans carry food, and these bears have become adept at acquiring it. Protect your provisions and pack. The ford of Mono Creek (not labeled on the topo map) is accomplished by a little rock-hopping. Beyond, the trail stays high above Illilouette Creek, and at one point we can look down into a narrow gorge, water-carved in the bedrock, with large water-worn potholes along its sides. Then the trail descends near the stream again to another good campsite. The shortcut to the Panorama Trail, shown on the topo map and labeled TRAIL, no longer exists. We now climb moderately up the canyon wall, away from the stream, and join the Panorama Trail, which ends at Glacier Point.

BACKPACK TRAIL #2

Wawona loop via Royal Arch and Chilnualna Lakes (30 miles; 41 eq. miles)

This route climbs past Chilnualna Falls to several high mountain lakes. Both stream and lake fishing can be good to excellent, and there are many good campsites.

There are two trailheads. The official trail, not shown on the topo map, leaves from a parking area behind the Wawona Ranger Station. Across the road is a sign reading *Chilnualna*

Falls 4.1 . . . . This trail parallels the main road a short distance, crosses a dirt service road, and then turns left away from the main road and ascends an old fire road. It then skirts the community of North Wawona, undulating wildly as it crosses numerous runoff stream beds—the kind of trail most backpackers detest. Another trail leaves from a private roadway where there is no parking area. Therefore, the authors suggest leaving the cars at the official trailhead, walking 1.4 miles up the Chilnualna Road (North Wawona Road) and turning left on Larke Lane. One block up this street is a sign, *Private—Cars and Motorcycles Prohibited.* Walk up this road past the sign for about 250 yards, to where a trail takes off on the right, going east. About half a mile up, this trail joins the one coming from the ranger station at an unmarked junction.

Beyond the junction, the combined trail ascends moderately under an open forest of ponderosa pines, incense-cedars, black oaks, canyon live oaks and an occasional Douglas-fir. There are clumps of very large manzanita bushes, and kit-kit-dizze forms a carpet over the forest floor. The dead lower branches of the cedar trees are beautifully decorated with green staghorn lichen. Occasionally, through the tops of the trees, we catch glimpses of Wawona Dome to the south.

About half a mile up from the junction, where the trail comes close to Chilnualna Creek, there is a pretty little waterfall—a good place for a refreshing drink and a short rest. Leaving the stream behind, the trail ascends the north canyon wall via a series of switchbacks. When we have almost gained the altitude of the top of the falls, we contour across a very rocky section of trail to them. This rocky section is open; and one gets good views into Wawona Valley and the wooded

ridges beyond. Turning a corner at the top of the fall we have
seen, we find another, even more spectacular one before us.
If these little-known falls were somewhere else other than in a
national park that has so many world-renowned falls, people
would travel hundreds of miles to view them. Above the falls
a lateral trail from the Buck Camp Trail near Turner Meadows
comes in on the left.

Beyond this junction our path descends to cross on footlogs
an unnamed tributary of Chilnualna Creek (campsites), then
climbs over a ridge to a boulder crossing of the main stream,
where there is a larger campsite. We continue climbing
through mixed forest, passing beautifully flowered meadows
and streamsides. It is pleasant to walk on this well-graded trail,
sometimes near a laughing, gurgling stream, sometimes high
along the canyon wall above it. Finally, 3.2 miles from the
last junction we join the Buck Camp Trail. Our route eastward
from here to the trail junction northwest of Buena Vista Lake,
seven miles away, is described in Backpack Trail #1.

Turning west at the latter junction, the trail leads gently
over a little ridge, then drops fairly steeply down a rocky hillside. Here one has extensive views westward of low, forested
mountains that typify the middle Sierra elevations. We soon
pass reed-bound Upper Chilnualna Lake, with a good campsite
and often good trout fishing. Down the trail we cross the outlet of another Chilnualna Lake, but the lake itself is hidden
from us. Beyond the outlet is a large, flat-floored valley, most
of it densely forested, which must have been a lake just after
the last glacier melted, and then a meadow. The trail divides
at the small remaining part of the meadow. To ensure dry
feet, go left (south) and skirt the meadow to Lower Chilnualna

Lake—another good camping and fishing spot. From here, short cross-country walks will take you to any of the other lakes in this group.

Continuing westward, we cross and recross the outlet stream of the lower lake, descending moderately. The flower gardens are almost continuous but the species in bloom change from the early-spring snow plants to the fall goldenrods. After crossing the main Chilnualna Creek, we follow its right bank down to the Buck Camp Trail. About 100 yards south of the crossing is a good campsite. Our route goes right (north) 0.8 mile to another junction, and then left (west) toward Wawona. We jump across the stream that drains Turner Meadows and climb up a broad ridge to an open viewpoint on top. On the descent into a forest containing sugar pines, their large, distinctive cones line the trail. Continuing the moderate-to-fairly-steep descent, we cross two more tributaries of Chilnualna Creek, finding many azaleas growing on the banks. These are boisterous streams, and where the trail parallels them we walk to the tune of their music. Beyond a bare granite slope, we meet the trail on which this trip began and descend 5.3 miles to our starting point near the Wawona Ranger Station.

BACKPACK TRAIL #3

Bridalveil Campground to Mono Meadow via Ostrander and Hart Lakes (partly cross-country)
(15 miles; 21 eq. miles)

From the parking lot on the Glacier Point Road about a mile east of the Bridalveil Campground entrance, the trail leads south past a gate into a fairly dense lodgepole-pine forest. The first part of this route, as far as Ostrander Lake, was a road until the early 1970s, so it is wide and never very steep. The old license plates high up on the trees are for skiers who use this route to the Ostrander Hut in winter. Near Lost Bear Meadow, 1.7 miles up-trail, a short lateral takes off west to the Buck Camp Trail. Beyond this junction we pass several small streams that are usually dry by midsummer, but each is nevertheless bordered by a garden of wildflowers until late summer. Another lateral west to the Buck Camp Trail begins 0.9 mile from the last junction. Soon we enter a predominantly fir forest, with an occasional Jeffrey pine. Much of the red-fir bark used for the famous Yosemite firefall was hauled out from this forest. (Until 1968 a mass of burning bark was pushed off the cliff at Glacier Point every night in summer.)

Continuing up the old road, we cross an open expanse of exfoliating granite and then parallel a small stream where one should have no difficulty finding at least 10 species of flowers. Our climb is moderate until we ascend a forested ridge. Just a few yards down the other side, one should leave the trail and go about 25 yards northeast to an excellent viewpoint. Down to the left we see the Royal Arches; above them to the east are North Dome and Basket Dome, and then Half Dome. Closer to us is Mt. Starr King, and in steps behind it are Clouds Rest and Mt. Hoffmann. Then come the peaks of the Tuolumne Meadows region, and farther east are all the peaks of the Clark Range, from Quartzite Peak to Merced Peak. Returning to the trail, we descend a short distance to beautiful, blue Ostrander Lake, backgrounded by the robust cliffs of Horse Ridge. Often in the summer a ranger lives in the hut here.

The hut is for use of the public only by reservation in the winter; however, there are numerous campsites around the lake.

From Ostrander Lake we begin a cross-country route by skirting the north end of the lake and climbing eastward past several small tarns. A ducked route to Hart Lake exists, but it isn't necessary to follow it. Just keep far enough north of Horse Ridge for easy walking, staying parallel to it. Toward the east end of Horse Ridge is Hart Lake, another lake to excite the photographer. There are good campsites here, and some trout for the lucky fisherman.

There are two routes northeast from Hart Lake to the Buena Vista Trail. One is down the lake's outlet stream. The other is a ducked route going north from Hart Lake, staying just west of the crest of a minor ridge. Once on the Buena Vista Trail, we follow the description in Backpack Trail #1 to the junction with the Mono Meadow Trail. At this junction our route turns west and climbs toward the Glacier Point Road. About halfway up, as we cross a rocky divide, we can look back and see fine views of the Mt. Starr King group of domes. The large dome to their left is the back side of Half Dome. Our trail now descends gently to cross Mono Creek via a good footlog and continues almost level for another mile to Mono Meadow. In early summer this boggy meadow can be by-passed by an unmarked horse trail that skirts it on the north. Beyond the meadow we make our last 400-foot climb to the Glacier Point Road. About 1.5 miles west on this road is the parking lot from which we started.

"The population bomb keeps ticking." Dr. Paul Ehrlich

BACKPACK TRAIL #4

Glacier Point to Half Dome
(10.2 miles; 16 eq. miles going; 13 eq. miles returning)

For many energetic visitors to Yosemite Valley, climbing
Half Dome is the height of their ambitions. Some try to make
the round trip from Happy Isles in one day. They focus on the
one-way distance of 8.2 miles, but the almost 5000-foot elevation gain makes the round trip 26 eq. miles, a strenuous one-
day hike. It is easier to take several days, and easier to start
from Glacier Point and end at Happy Isles.

See Day Hike #14 for a description of the trail to Nevada
Fall. Only 0.2 mile beyond the bridge at the top of the fall,
the foot trail from Happy Isles joins our route. We then climb
over a shoulder of Liberty Cap, through mountain chaparral
and then through a sparse forest of Jeffrey and sugar pine.
Liberty Cap can be climbed from the top of this shoulder;
the greatest difficulty is getting through the brush when you
leave the trail. At the approach to Little Yosemite Valley is a
trail junction. The unmarked left fork, a shortcut, offers little
shade; the right fork, marked *Merced Lake Trail*, is much
pleasanter. A half mile up the right fork our trail, the John
Muir Trail, turns left (north), and soon it climbs fairly steeply
on sandy switchbacks. An open forest of black oaks, ponderosa and sugar pines, and incense-cedars provides some shade,
but this climb can be uncomfortably hot on a summer afternoon. About 1.5 miles (3.5 eq. miles) up this slope, the Half
Dome Trail leaves the John Muir Trail. Another half mile up
the Muir Trail, at its junction with the Clouds Rest Trail, there

are several good campsites.

Turning left (north) onto the Half Dome Trail, we continue our moderate climb. A short half mile up this trail a side trail goes right about 25 yards to a small spring. A short distance farther up our route, another trail to the right goes about 200 yards to several good campsites. (There is water just beyond the camps.) These make good base camps from which to climb Half Dome.

As we proceed up the trail, the forest becomes more open, and we get views of the surrounding mountains. Approaching the northeast shoulder of Half Dome, the trail becomes a series of steep granite steps, which should be climbed slowly in this rarefied air. Notice that trees are growing on this seemingly solid rock. Topping the shoulder we see the cables on Half Dome which will help us on the final climb. At the bottom of the cables a sign reads: *Notice—It is dangerous to use cables during lightning storms.* Furthermore, if cumulus clouds are in the neighborhood, extreme caution should be used, as they can move above the dome fairly rapidly and produce an electric storm. If you hear thunder in the distance, don't climb up. If you hear it while on the summit, descend the cables as quickly as possible. Strong electrical charges build up on them even though the lightning storm may be miles away.

The two cables, about three feet apart, are supported at waist height by upright pipes emplaced in the rock. At the base of most pairs of pipes is a 2-by-4 cross step to rest on. Looking up the cables from the bottom may be scary, but the climb is essentially safe, as thousands every year can testify. Climb slowly and rest often to make the ascent enjoyable.

The view from the top is all-encompassing. All the sur-

rounding mountains can be seen: Mt. Hoffmann is the impressive peak on the skyline to the north; northeast, Clouds Rest looms up closely; eastward are the peaks of the Cathedral Range; and directly east Mt. Florence blots out most of Mts. Maclure and Lyell; southeast are the peaks of the Clark Range; Mt. Starr King is almost straight south, with the Buena Vista Crest and Horse Ridge above it in the distance. Westward, Glacier Point commands the view, and of course the meadows, forests and roads of Yosemite Valley below are laid out like a full-scale map. It looks as if one could spit into Mirror Lake, but don't try—sometimes there are rock climbers coming up the face.

The descent of the cables should be made slowly, resting several times. If a car shuttle can be arranged or a connection made with the once-a-day bus, you can shorten the trip by returning to Happy Isles rather than to Glacier Point.

BACKPACK TRAIL #5

Mono Meadow to Little Yosemite
(8 miles; 9 eq. miles going; 11 eq. miles returning)

This is an easy backpack trip and one that could be started in late afternoon, since there are campsites less than two hours from the trailhead. The trail starts from the Glacier Point Road about 2.5 miles east of the Bridalveil Campground entrance road. There is ample parking at the trailhead but no camping. From the road, the trail drops 400 feet in the first half mile, to the flats of Mono Meadow. In early season one can cross this boggy meadow without getting wet feet by tak-

ing the unmarked horse trail around the north side. Beyond
the meadow we cross Mono Creek on good footlogs and climb
gently over the shoulder of a broad ridge. From its crest there
are good views across the canyon of Illilouette Creek to the
Mt. Starr King group of domes. The large dome to the left of
this group is the back side of Half Dome.

The flower-bordered trail then descends moderately across
granite slopes and through pleasant, open forests. Near the
bottom of the canyon we meet the Buena Vista Trail, turn
right on it for 50 yards, and then turn left down to Illilouette
Creek. There are campsites on both sides of the stream, but
wood is scarce. We ford the creek, the best place being about
50 yards upstream. Use extreme caution during high water.

A short way up the east bank is a junction. The trail to the
southeast (upstream) goes to Ottoway Lakes, Red Peak Pass,
Moraine Meadow, and other points east and south. For
descriptions of these routes see the High Sierra Hiking Guide
to *Merced Peak*. We go north, downstream, across a sandy
meadow and, after jumping a small, unnamed stream, climb
moderately to what is shown on the topo map as the Mono
Meadow Trail. This is a misnomer, as we have just come over
the trail from Mono Meadow, and it should carry that name.
We continue northward on this trail, cross a low, forested
saddle, and descend to the blacktop Panorama Trail that
comes up from Glacier Point. A mile of moderate descent
brings us to the John Muir Trail, coming up from Happy Isles.
We turn right toward Nevada Fall, and after a 0.2-mile gentle
descent we cross the Merced River on a bridge at the brink of
the fall. To our left, beyond the bridge, is an overlook directly
above the fall, and when the river is flowing full, the roar of

the fall and the spray plumes leaping out into the air defy description.

Continuing eastward, we pass a foot trail that comes up from the top of Vernal Fall and swings around a shoulder of Liberty Cap. Approaching Little Yosemite Valley, we meet a trail fork. The unsigned left trail is a shortcut to Half Dome, Clouds Rest and points beyond. We keep right, staying near the river. At the next junction the John Muir Trail turns left (north), bound for Tuolumne Meadows and eventually Mt. Whitney. The surrounding area is a very popular camping area. There are chemical toilets here, and wood is scarce. Little Yosemite Valley is about 3 miles long, and the farther one penetrates, the less dense is the population. A word of caution about food in this valley—the bears have learned that humans carry many goodies that bears enjoy. The authors have camped here occasionally for over 35 years and have seen each generation of bears growing smarter at outwitting the camper and stealing his food. Protect *all* packs!

For the return journey, one may elect to shorten the trip by descending to Happy Isles, if one can arrange a car shuttle or connect with the once-a-day bus that goes to Glacier Point.

LATERAL TRAIL #1

Deer Camp Trail from Alder Creek Trail to Buck Camp Trail
(3½ miles; 6 eq. miles traveling east)

This short trail connects the Alder Creek and Buck Camp trails. A fire road from Chinquapin meets the trail about midpoint, at Deer Camp.

Starting from the west end of this lateral, at the Alder Creek Trail, we cross Alder Creek on footlogs upstream from the trail ford. A steady, moderate climb is relieved by a couple of stream crossings, and there is abundant wildlife along this little-used trail. You may be startled by a covey of grouse flying noisily up and away, or you may be fortunate enough to have a mother quail play the broken-wing trick, flopping along to lead you away from her covey of chicks. The name "Deer Camp" may give the impression of a good campsite. However, this place at the junction of trail and fire road was formerly a lumber camp when this area was a private holding within the Park boundaries. Remains of old buildings, fences, dumps, surface pipes and other litter make the place unappealing as a camping site. It should and probably will be cleaned out within a few years.

Continuing eastward from Deer Camp, the trail climbs into less dense forest, where we can look back and see Deer Camp below, as well as the canyon of the South Fork Merced River beyond. About a mile from Deer Camp, the trail tops a ridge, approaches a meadow, and forks. The left fork is a packer's shortcut and is not maintained. The main trail goes right, across the stream and around the south side of the meadow.

"Time is a strange standard of measure, for its value changes so much, depending on what you're doing and where you are . . . in the woods . . . Time is a snow storm, a downpour of rain . . . In nature time doesn't trot right along. Often it stops for a while and sometimes backtracks on its own trail." Rowlands, *Cache Lake Country*

At the head of this long meadow we meet the Buck Camp
Trail (Backpack Trail #1).

LATERAL TRAIL #2

McGurk Meadow Trail from Bridalveil Campground to the Pohono Trail (3 miles)

This trail makes a good day hike from a base at Bridalveil
Campground. The route can be made even shorter by starting
from the Glacier Point Road, where the trail crosses the road
0.2 mile west of the campground entrance. There is no parking area at the trail crossing, but there are wide shoulders a
short distance in each direction.

Starting from the phone booth at the campground entrance,
proceed west on the blacktop of the old Glacier Point Road.
After crossing Peregoy Meadow, we leave the old road and
take a trail going north, paralleling the meadow. We climb
over a low, rocky ridge where large boulders are perched on
the bare granite. These boulders were carried here by glaciers
thousands of years ago, and were left when the ice melted.
Descending from the ridge, we cross the Glacier Point Road,
and about a mile farther come to large, beautifully flowered
McGurk Meadow. A plank bridge provides the crossing for a
stream flowing through the meadow.

Beyond the meadow, the trail climbs gently over a low
ridge and then descends to its junction with the Pohono Trail.
A short distance east of this junction there are campsites on
Bridalveil Creek.

Climbers

EVEN AS BACKPACKERS ARE considered serious individualists, climbers have a reputation of snobbery. Far from being the stereotyped daredevil, the usual climber is addicted to methodical disciplines, and not all of his climbs are made over thousands of feet of air while hanging by his fingernails—indeed, *most* of the very difficult climbs in Yosemite Valley are less than 1000 feet long.

Climbs are rated by their difficulty, beginning with Class 1 and progressing through Class 6. Class 1 is trail and easy cross-country; Class 2 is easy scrambling; Class 3 is scrambling up slopes using your hands as well as your feet. Class 4 requires a rope for safety; Class 5 requires pitons and/or nuts for protection; and Class 6 requires nylon loops to put your feet in. Climbs are also classified by the average time it takes to complete them: from Grade I, a few hours to Grade VI, several days.

The following list is compiled of the peaks within the *Yosemite* quadrangle which are Class 1 or Class 2:

El Capitan (from the north)
Eagle Peak
Sentinel Dome
Buena Vista Peak
Mt. Starr King (except for the 4th-class summit dome)

Wawona Dome
Liberty Cap (northeast slope)
the Diving Board (from Little Yosemite Valley)
Half Dome (if you stay between the cables)

Routes of Class 3 to Class 6 are described in Steve Roper's *Climber's Guide to Yosemite Valley.* Those intending to do such climbs should check in first at the Park headquarters.

BIBLIOGRAPHY

Books

Adams, Ansel and Virginia. *Illustrated Guide to Yosemite.* San Francisco: Sierra Club, 1963.

Farquhar, Francis. *History of the Sierra Nevada.* Berkeley: U.C. Press, 1965.

Matthes, Francois (edited by Fritiof Fryxell). *The Incomparable Valley.* Berkeley: U.C. Press, 1964.

Muir, John. *The Yosemite.* Berkeley: U.C. Press, 1963.

Munz, Philip A. *California Mountain Wildflowers.* Berkeley: U.C. Press, 1963.

Munz, Philip A., and David Keck. *A California Flora.* Berkeley and Los Angeles: U.C. Press, 1968.

Murie, Olaus. *Field Guide to Animal Tracks.* Boston: Houghton, 1958.

Paden, Irene, and Margaret Schlichtmann. *The Big Oak Flat Road to Yosemite.* Yosemite: Yosemite Natural History Association, 1959.

Parsons, Mary. *Wild Flowers of California.* New York: Dover Publications, 1966.

Peterson, Roger. *A Field Guide to Western Birds.* Boston: Houghton, 1968.

Russell, Carl P. *100 Years in Yosemite.* Yosemite: Yosemite Natural History Association, 1968.

Storer, Tracy, and Robert Usinger. *Sierra Nevada Natural History.* Berkeley: U.C. Press, 1963.

Sudworth, George. *Forest Trees of the Pacific Slope.* New York: Dover Publications, 1967.

Cathedral Spires   *Thomas Winnett*

Pamphlets

California Division of Mines and Geology. *Geologic Guide
    to the Merced Canyon and Yosemite Valley (Bull. 182).*
Hood, Mary and Bill. *Yosemite Wildflowers.* Yosemite:
    Flying Spur Press, 1969.
Matthes, Francois. *Geologic History of Yosemite Valley.*
    U.S. Geological Survey, 1930.
Thomas, Winnie, and Hasse Bunnell. *Food for Knapsackers.*
    San Francisco: Sierra Club, 1971.
Yosemite Natural History Association.
    Fishes of Yosemite
    Cone-Bearing Trees of Yosemite National Park
    Broad-leaved Trees of Yosemite National Park
    Wawona's Yesterdays
    Wildflowers of the Sierra
    Mammals of Yosemite National Park
    Birds of Yosemite
    The Tioga Road
    A Brief Story of the Geology of Yosemite Valley
    Yosemite Indians

Related Wilderness Press Publications

Rowell, Galen A., ed. *The Vertical World of Yosemite.* 1974.
Schaffer, Jeffrey P. *et al. The Pacific Crest Trail.*
Winnett, Thomas. *Sierra North.*
Winnett, Thomas. *The Tahoe-Yosemite Trail.*

plus *High Sierra Hiking Guides* to other quadrangles in
Yosemite National Park: *Hetch Hetchy, Merced Peak,
Tuolumne Meadows.*

Index